"*Authenticity at Your Best* is a must read for anyone seeking a more expansive and freer expression of who they are. Ann Allen's vast knowledge and experience is reflected in this incredibly important book on discovering and uncovering your true self. Ann demonstrates through her own life how she made decisions, choosing to follow her heart, instead of following her fears and bending to the will of others. She shares that the best version of ourselves requires we make tough choices, to not abandon ourselves or our own guidance. When we step into our truth, the universe shifts and provides immediate evidence to confirm we have made the right choice. If you are struggling with self-worth and hiding your true potential, *Authenticity at Your Best* will free you from self-sabotage so the world can greatly benefit."

— Deborah Reynolds, Speaker, Image and Transformation Expert, and Co-Author with Wayne Dyer and Tony Robbins of *Wake up, Live the Life You Love: Living in Clarity*

"Have you ever been frustrated operating a complicated piece of equipment for which you have no owner's manual? You've figured a lot of things out on your own using trial and error, but you just know you're not getting the best possible results. Well, Ann Allen's *Authenticity at Your Best* is the owner's manual for life that you've been missing. It is a workbook that guides you in how to show up mentally, emotionally, and spiritually to create your best life experience. Many authors preach the magic way; by contrast, Ann invites the reader on a guided exploration of what's working, what isn't, and what to do about it. I'd want this book with me if I were stranded on an island."

— Cyndi Hacker, Owner of The Coaching Staff/ Excellence in Leadership and Personal Effectiveness

"In clear, concise, yet loving language, Ann Allen provides a simple yet powerful handbook to getting to know yourself better. No matter your age or how much you have read, there are gems in this book to assist you in delving deeper for self-examination and growth. *Authenticity at Your Best* is a book to keep with you, filled with information, thoughts, examples, and tools. It is presented with love, encouragement, optimism, and enduring respect for the challenges of being human. I love this book, and I learn something or discover a new aspect of myself and life each time I pick it up. Every once in a while, a book comes into your hands that seems to be written just for you. This book is a loving reminder of all the ways we are a product of our lives, and it gives us reason to review and celebrate."

— Holly Thomas, Artist

"A thought-provoking, inspiring guide. During these times, get back to basics. Authenticity will set you apart from others, guiding you back to your true self."

— Maura Zazenski, Co-Chair, Marketing and Public Relations

"Ann Allen's *Authenticity at Your Best* is a great read. It made me think about who I am and, more importantly, at age sixty-seven, who I want to be. It helped me open my eyes to the things I do to prevent me from being my authentic self, and it gave me the tools to start changing. Ms. Allen uses many examples that describe how we can identify unhealthy patterns and start letting them go."

— Cheryl Garcia, Littleton, Colorado

"A rich, insightful, and personal reflection on the nature of sustainable happiness. Ann Allen has given us a guide to finding our true and authentic self."

— **Sharon Sekeres, Valencia, California**

"As a young twenty-year-old, I found *Authenticity at Your Best* to be a wonderful guide to understanding and living a purposeful, authentic life."

— **Cole DeLeon, Northridge, California**

"In *Authenticity at Your Best*, Ann Allen engages us by laying out personal examples of discovering the path of self-understanding, growth, and healing, which lead to the realization of the true authentic self. She helps us discover our limiting/false beliefs, repeatable patterns, emotional wounds, etc., and sets a trajectory of releasing what is keeping us stuck from living our authentic self. Ann Allen provides a well-written, thought-provoking guide for anyone undertaking change in their life. If you are living in a state of questioning, growing, and wanting more, this book is a wonderful guide and supportive tool you will be sure to reference over and over."

— **Sue Keller, Wholistic Energy Practitioner**

"*Authenticity at Your Best* is insightful and challenges you to dive deeper into your self-awareness. If you are looking to grow and connect with your authentic self, this book is a great read!"

— **Katy Williamson, Yoga Instructor**

"In this powerful and dynamic book, Ann Allen speaks with wisdom and practicality. She offers a helpful guide for navigating the internal struggle to be true to ourselves and others. Through the exercises at the end of each chapter, she provides guidance to help align our values with an understanding of our true self. *Authenticity at Your Best* is a 'must-read' for anyone committed to their own personal and professional growth."

— Susan Friedmann, CSP, International Bestselling Author of *Riches in Niches: How to Make It BIG in a small Market*

"Ann Allen shows us that if we truly want to create our own destiny, first we must be authentic. Otherwise, we will live our lives following someone else's destiny. Her advice on developing awareness and manifesting your vision is alone worth the price of this book, and there are so many more gems to glean riches from."

— Patrick Snow, Publishing Coach and International Best-Selling Author of *Creating Your Own Destiny* and *Boy Entrepreneur*

"I absolutely loved this book! Ann Allen's years of experience, study, and research have led her to write a book that is a simple, understandable guide to living our most authentic life. The questions at the end of each chapter invite the reader to honestly search for their own truth with love and compassion for self and others. I have known and admired Ann for years, and I recognize her voice on every page. I felt as if I were having a conversation with Ann as I read this book. For more than thirty years I have been a mental health therapist, and I have never read anything that more succinctly and clearly outlines the barriers to living an authentic life. I will enthusiastically recommend *Authenticity at Your Best* to family, friends, and patients."

— **Sandra Davis McEntire, PhD, Psychologist**

"*Authenticity at Your Best* sends a clear message that if you aren't authentic, you really aren't anything. Too often we find ourselves tossed about by life's storms, but Ann shows us that when we become clear on who we are, we can create a solid foundation of authenticity that will not falter when the winds of change blow."

— **Tyler R. Tichelaar, PhD and Award-Winning Author of *Narrow Lives* and *The Gothic Wanderer***

"In this time of great challenges, many are searching for guidance, direction, understanding, courage, and feeling connected to family, to others, and to themselves. *Authenticity at Your Best* is a treasure for those searching, and it stands above so many spiritual books because it is authentic! Ann Allen, whom I have known for years, instructs the reader on how to achieve their own personal truth by presenting personal and real stories, challenging thought questions, and simple, yet powerful and effective exercises. She motivates the reader to continue their journey, and the ending affirmations are a perfect conclusion to her brilliantly written book."

— **Rob Wergin, Divine Conduit as seen in the documentary *HEAL***

AUTHENTICITY AT YOUR BEST

How to discover and uncover
"your true self"

ANN ALLEN

AVIVA
PUBLISHING
New York

Dedication

To my children, Tommy and Sarah, who have been my
greatest teachers on this journey of becoming.

. . .

To my parents, who gave me the foundation from which
I sprang in order to expand and grow.

. . .

To you, the reader, who seeks to heighten your awareness
and live a life more joy-filled and free.

Acknowledgments

I would like to thank Michele Williams for her support in helping me express my thoughts in a meaningful way. Her grasp of the material and her writing skills were so essential for the completion of this book.

. . .

A special thanks to Anne Hood for her support on so many levels to make this book possible.

. . .

Thank you, Jane Fisher, for assisting with the initial editing and format. Jane worked tirelessly getting each chapter organized and easier to read. I am so grateful.

. . .

Additional thanks to Holly Thomas, Sandra MacEntire, Cyndi Hacker, Sue and Paul Keller, Celia Coats, Margy Gresham, Kathy Green, and Sarah Hoenninger for your support and encouragement.

. . .

Jack Stucki, thank you for your amazing sessions that have grounded, balanced, and helped heal my body and soul. Your work has been so essential to my awareness and growth, and I deeply appreciate you, your work, and your friendship.

. . .

Judy Stucki, thank you for your friendship and support. It has been incredibly valuable to me. And an additional thanks for all you give to enhance Jack's sessions and help make the entire experience so exceptional.

. . .

Rob Wergin, your incredible gift of allowing the Divine to come through you as well as your tireless effort to assist so many is an inspiration. My soul cherishes the amazing healing I have had as a result of your work. I am so grateful.

. . .

Patrick Snow, I am so appreciative of your incredible skill and coaching to assist in launching this book.

Contents

The Invitation

Oriah Mountain Dreamer

It doesn't interest me
what you do for a living.
I want to know
what you ache for
and if you dare to dream
of meeting your heart's longing.
It doesn't interest me
how old you are.
I want to know
if you will risk
looking like a fool
for love
for your dream
for the adventure of being alive.
It doesn't interest me
what planets are
squaring your moon...
I want to know
if you have touched
the centre of your own sorrow
if you have been opened

by life's betrayals
or have become shrivelled and closed
from fear of further pain.
I want to know
if you can sit with pain
mine or your own
without moving to hide it
or fade it
or fix it.
I want to know
if you can be with joy
mine or your own
if you can dance with wildness
and let the ecstasy fill you
to the tips of your fingers and toes
without cautioning us
to be careful
to be realistic
to remember the limitations
of being human.
It doesn't interest me
if the story you are telling me
is true.
I want to know if you can
disappoint another
to be true to yourself.
If you can bear
the accusation of betrayal

and not betray your own soul.
If you can be faithless
and therefore trustworthy.
I want to know if you can see Beauty
even when it is not pretty
every day.
And if you can source your own life
from its presence.
I want to know
if you can live with failure
yours and mine
and still stand at the edge of the lake
and shout to the silver of the full moon,
"Yes."
It doesn't interest me
to know where you live
or how much money you have.
I want to know if you can get up
after the night of grief and despair
weary and bruised to the bone
and do what needs to be done
to feed the children.
It doesn't interest me
who you know
or how you came to be here.
I want to know if you will stand
in the centre of the fire

with me
and not shrink back.
It doesn't interest me
where or what or with whom
you have studied.
I want to know
what sustains you
from the inside
when all else falls away.
I want to know
if you can be alone
with yourself
and if you truly like
the company you keep
in the empty moments.

Foreword

by Jack Stucki

One of our prisons on this planet is that we have been made to think we are our brain. Ann Allen had a vision to assist people to become free. This book is the materialization of her vision. She wants to help humanity in this time of chaos and uncertainty. Ann dreamed about giving a gift—the gift of encouraging each of us to become our true selves, free from the distractions that burden us. She felt in her heart that we can learn lessons about shaping and healing our minds and our bodies, that we can grow to know our spirits, so we can truly continue our paths through life with honesty and integrity, not only for ourselves, but also for all those around us.

For more than thirty years, I have known Ann both professionally and spiritually. She exemplifies an authentic life by living every day as her true self. She knows how important it is to live with integrity and authenticity, and she desires that way of living for each and every human being. She has taken great care to point out the many distractions—some of them subtle—that can divert us from living authentically. At the time a distraction occurs, it may feel good to us. It can feel like an easier way to display our personality or create our public image—an easier way to be accepted or, at least, not to be shunned by others. Often, we choose that easier way instead of honestly presenting ourselves as we truly are. The only real you is the honest you—we can feel good, inside and outside, while being our true selves instead of presenting ourselves as someone we really are not.

Ann gently presents the reader with the various distractions that keep us from being authentic, helping us to identify aspects of the distracted self. She describes each distraction and offers honest guidance to help us overcome it. She presents ways we can be and feel good about the authentic *self*.

This book flows seamlessly from beginning to end. It is easy to read and very engaging as it offers us, the readers, encouragement on our paths to becoming authentic humans living full lives that benefit us and the whole world.

"And this above all—to thine own self be true."

— WILLIAM SHAKESPEARE, *HAMLET*, ACT I, SCENE 3

Jack Stucki, RMT, BCIAC, is a Subtle Energy Medicine pioneer. He is the co-founder of the Merkaba Research and Healing Center and a former three-term president of the Colorado Association for Applied Psychophysiology and Biofeedback. Jack has also taught courses on various topics including integrative medicine at several universities, and his work has been featured in numerous books. Jack is the recipient of national and international awards, including the Johann Stoyva Award for outstanding contributions to biofeedback.

What If

— JUNE C. MILLER

What if I was me
And no one else
And nothing changed
Yet everything changed
Just from being who I am.
And what if I laughed
And knew I finally got it right
With my yes and my no
Following only me
And being one-of-a kind
I added to this world
The only thing I had to give
And found the world had need
Of another true me.
It's only a what-if for now
At least, in the now of yesterday.
Today is the now of eternity
And what else can there be
But me being me
And living me
And laughing at who
I thought I had to be
Yesterday.

Introduction

Authenticity

*"The moment in between what you once were,
and who are now becoming, is where the
dance of life really takes place."*

— BARBARA DE ANGELIS

Authenticity is an often overused word that is rarely understood. Many would define authenticity as "being honest" or "telling the truth." It encompasses so very much more. It is best defined as a congruency between the inside and outside worlds. Your inside world is your beliefs and values, your feelings, your gifts and talents, your passions and dreams, and your challenges and experiences. Your outside world is work, home, community, play, and life.

Before reading further, ask yourself:

- Do I live my beliefs and values?

- Am I sharing my gifts and talents?

- What dreams have I forgotten?
- What passion still wants to be expressed?

The scope of authenticity is so much more extensive than you previously may have imagined, and when it is fully expressed, the "real" person shows up. When you are free of limiting beliefs and harmful patterns, the true and beautiful parts of you reveal themselves. Real connection can then begin on a level not possible before.

What does authenticity mean to you?

My hope is this book brings a more expanded meaning to your answer.

Please join me in this journey of exploration as we strive to understand and become truly authentic in our lives.

Ann Allen

Chapter 1

Grasping the Full Meaning
of Authenticity

*"We're really afraid to show who we are to
one another, not only our weakness, but also
our strength and our beauty."*

— ELIZABETH LESSER

"This other work you're doing is just too unusual. People aren't ready for it. Doctors aren't ready. If they know you're doing it, we're worried they won't refer patients to any of us. Unless you stop doing it, we'll have to ask you to leave the group."

I stared back in disbelief at the woman who had just delivered this blow. Where had this come from?

"I'm sorry, Ann," the woman continued gently. "We all agree on this."

Only six months earlier, a member of this outstanding group of successful biofeedback professionals had personally reached out to invite me to join their small collective. They had banded together with an intention to market their work to the insurance companies and doctors in our area. At the time, I was recognized as both a biofeedback and Neuro-Link therapist. I had a positive reputation and maintained a thriving practice that already served many insurance companies' clients. It seemed I was a good fit.

Since I had joined their group, we had spent countless hours together in meetings and over the phone. We planned. We strategized. For months, we discussed and debated and considered. But not once had anyone dropped even the faintest hint that the work known as Neuro-Link, which I did in addition to biofeedback therapy, would pose a problem for the group.

Now, just weeks before our marketing materials would go out, they were dropping a bombshell.... Neuro-Link seemed too weird for them. They didn't want their names connected with it in any way. To be fair, I could understand their perspective. At the time, biofeedback therapy seemed "out there" to most of the people I encountered. When I enrolled my son in a new school in Denver, their staff psychologist, a professional with twenty years of experience, shared that I was the first parent in the biofeedback profession to have a child in their school.

Even my own mother once asked, "Why would anyone pay you to get them relaxed?" Never mind that she knew I had a master's degree in this field from San Francisco State University. I simply replied, "You know those awful migraine headaches you get, Mom? What if my work could help you control them? Would it be worth it then?" Suddenly, she understood. She never questioned biofeedback therapy again.

Now, after many years of patience and careful explanations of my work, biofeedback had gained enough credibility for me to build a healthy practice that included referrals from medical doctors. I remained surprised by the number of seemingly intelligent people I encountered who said they knew little or nothing about biofeedback, and plenty of those who had heard of it still continued to think of it as a little "out there."

Neuro-Link, however, made the practice of biofeedback look normal, even tame, to many. A modality developed by the New Zealand osteopath Dr. Allan Phillips, Neuro-Link is a complex system that aims to assess and address the reasons the brain has failed. It then helps the body to restore homeostasis to function normally. Neuro-Link requires assessing and treating the body in a very gentle and holistic approach.

Like my colleagues, I had felt skeptical of Neuro-Link at first. But the principles behind Dr. Phillips' research resonated with me. The system testified to the human brain's adeptness and complexity. At a time when computers were becoming more popular than ever, I saw the brain as the greatest computer in the world, and I felt Neuro-Link was a way to tap into its incredible potential. The more I explored it, the more passionate I became about this gentle technique that produced profound results with my clients. In many ways, it was its own feedback system.

In the days following that fateful meeting in which the group informed me of their collective opinion regarding Neuro-Link, my dilemma with them filled my mind. I found myself wondering if I should give it up. The practical part of me screamed that I should go along with the crowd and let go of Neuro-Link. After all, I was the sole financial support not just for myself but also for my two young children. If the group's marketing efforts worked as well as they hoped, they could possibly capture all the insurance business in the area. If I didn't remain a part of their association, I could potentially find myself with no clients in a heartbeat. I had no ethical obligation to continue this work, so why risk so much to keep doing it?

On the other hand, I knew I had a skill that would help many in pain. I had already experienced my work helping so many more people when I combined the two modalities. Therefore, I knew I could personally accomplish more if I continued to use Neuro-Link as an adjunct to biofeedback. I couldn't give up on it, not yet. I proposed a solution I thought could work for everyone. "What if I offered the 10-12 sessions that an insurance company pays for as biofeedback, only giving clients the option to experience Neuro-Link afterwards, on their own dime?" I felt this would surely work for everyone in the group since I would not be overtly advertising the technique they questioned.

"Ann," the group's leader told me, "we think the technique probably works. We just can't take the risk." Others agreed. Giving up this technique remained the only way they would allow me to market my services with them. Clearly, I would have to make a choice.

Many times during our earth-bound journey, life forces us to make choices like this one. Choices that might come unexpectedly and often seem unfair. We find ourselves confronted by the question, "Why has life pressed me between two seemingly undesirable options?" Rather than railing against this phenomenon, I prefer to see it as a natural part of the growing process we all must experience during our journey to be and become authentic.

My best definition of "authenticity" reflects balance: *When your inner world remains congruent with your outer world.* In other words, everything I believe is true for me—my beliefs, my thoughts, my feelings—must agree with how I exhibit this truth in my actions in my outer world. I have found this version of authenticity to be far from understood. Many define authenticity as "being honest or telling the truth." The kind of authenticity I'm talking about resides less in one particular kind of external expression and more in how well you live and express your own natural leanings.

I have shared this personal story because it beautifully illustrates the kind of dilemma life often provides to help us become more authentic. I had to decide if I would follow my heart and continue my work with Neuro-Link, or if I would follow my fears and bend to the group's will. In the end, I decided to leave the group. I felt truly frightened I might lose my practice, the sole source of income for my family. Would we survive without this support? I didn't know. But staying in the group would force me to abandon myself as well as my own guidance. I knew I could not risk that.

The universe's response to my decision amazed me. When I left the group, I was surprised when my phone began ringing off the hook. I knew the universe supported my decision so I would not need to worry about supporting my family. Several physicians who referred clients to me loved the technique and took the opportunity to experience the enjoyable resolution of pain in such a gentle way for themselves.

As we begin our exploration of authenticity, I would first like to talk about your inherent uniqueness. To find your uniqueness, you don't have to search very hard. Brain waves, fingerprints, DNA, the sound of your voice—all of these patterns belong only to you. You and you alone have faced the unique challenges of your life, relying on a combination of talents and gifts solely your own. God designed each of us this way, as one-of-a-kind expressions of divinity.

Many talk about this uniqueness, yet we constantly get bombarded with messages about how to dress, how to think, how to behave, and how to feel. Someone labeled "different" frequently gets bullied or shut out. Places where uniqueness is actually nourished and encouraged can be hard to find. Because of this pressure to conform, you may decide to give up on your own uniqueness as a way to survive. How often do you forfeit the precious gift of your unique self in order to fit in or claim an identity that makes you feel safe? At what cost? Author and Buddhist monk Jack Kornfield once said, "I think the greatest wound we've all experienced is somehow being rejected for being our most authentic self. And as a result of that, we try to be what we are not to get approval, love, protection, safety, money, whatever."

To understand this great need to be authentic, look at life as a great symphony. Only you can play your unique instrument. Without the music of your soul blending with all the others, something essential gets lost in life's expression of itself.

Being unique may mean you will sometimes have to go against the grain. Promptings from your own heart and mind don't always match up with the messages of the outside world. Staying true to them requires both stamina and faith in the process of being and becoming an authentic human being.

> "The ultimate care of the soul is being identified with the life that wants to live through you."
>
> — THOMAS MOORE

For everyone, the central business of life is to be a real person. But you don't arrive at this in one step. Rather, you continually engage in the ongoing process of becoming real.

I remember my own childhood. Growing up Catholic meant Catholic schools, Mass every Sunday, as well as learning and following the catechism. I tried hard to be a good Catholic girl. I followed the teachings I received with a pure heart, living the beliefs as authentically as I could. I also questioned many things I learned about the Catholic teachings as time went on. I simply wanted explanations that resonated with me as truth.

As I learned and discovered more about my own connection with the Divine and my faith, I also experienced the joy of discovery. Step by step, I was uncovering a philosophy of life that fit me. During this time, I laid the foundation for the spiritual path on which I have lived my life ever since.

I have always been drawn to the cutting edge of what is happening in the teaching world as well as in other areas of my life. I began my career teaching orthopedically challenged children in a progressive program in Champaign, Illinois, that integrated my students into the regular classroom. At the time, only a handful of schools were bringing challenged children into mainstream classrooms. I believed in this work wholeheartedly.

Many years later, my own inner promptings led me to get my master's in biofeedback and holistic health. These were cutting-edge fields at the time. I knew life would be different. Although teaching had always been a part of all my careers in many different fashions, this new career meant leaving a safe and acceptable teaching career to embark into a relatively unknown field in the '80s that was considered way out of the norm by many of my associates.

Throughout my life, I have frequently explored and reinvented my own authentic connection with the world around me. Something that felt very authentic to me in my thirties no longer fits now that I am in my eighties. I can look back at the past versions of myself and laugh at how I have changed. But I also honor all of them because I know each has reflected my best expression in the outer world of my changing inner landscape at the time.

The same holds true for each of us. Authenticity does not require you to nail things down, once and for all. You do not need to get your beliefs "figured out" or "right." Rather, life calls you to get right with yourself, as you are right now. *It beckons you to make decisions about your life not based in fear, as many do and I also have done from time to time, but from faith in your unique and essential expression as you.*

Being authentic means connecting with your inner wisdom and assuming responsibility for your life. It means connecting with the essence of what is inside you and honoring your gifts, talents, and dreams. By listening to yourself, you tune into passions, intuition, and Spirit.

These things might seem small compared to the pressing concerns of money, survival, prestige, or even the simple challenge of scheduling your day. Yet they are infinitely more powerful than any of these. As American philosopher Ralph Waldo Emerson wrote, "What lies behind us and what lies before us are tiny matters compared to what lies within." Some examples of not living authentically include:

- I need to be around nature to rejuvenate, but I never have time.

- I believe meditation is essential to living a balanced life, but when I sit down to meditate my mind won't stop, so I quit.

- I think it is important to recycle, but I always forget.I love to sing and share my voice, but I can't find a choir.

As you can see, lack of authenticity creeps in on us in many different forms. American author Stephen Pressfield noted, "Most of us have two lives. The life we live and the unlived life within us. Between the two stands resistance."

This book explores authenticity from a few different angles. I will take you through your inner world of Needs, Feelings, Beliefs, Passion, Dreams, Gifts, and Talents, exploring how authentically you relate to and express yourself in each of these areas. I will also explore the outer world of Home, Work, Community, Play, Relationships, and Life. The most important part of understanding your relationship with these two worlds is answering the question, "Are they congruent?"

Why should you take the time for an in-depth exploration of the topic of authenticity? Two reasons: Happiness and Freedom. I believe we feel most alive when we live a life that is true to who we are. Winning the lottery would be nice, and getting recognized professionally for your hard work feels great, but both pale in comparison to a healthy relationship with yourself. I believe nothing compares to a life dedicated to the pursuit of authenticity.

Information and practical questions are provided to help you assess and access your own authenticity. To illustrate each principle, I share stories from my life and the lives of coworkers. I encourage you to delve deeply into the questions asked and use this book as a tool to uncover your true authentic self.

To begin the process, set your intention for authenticity *now*. Expressing who you are is one of the greatest forms of healing I know. To help you set a clear intention for the healing journey this book outlines, I offer the following meditation.

Intention Meditation

Close your eyes. Now breathe deeply into your heart. Breathe into your very core. Feel your heart expand and your body relax.

As you hear the names of various muscle groups, notice any tension in each, and breathe into these areas, relaxing each muscle group.

Start with the forehead, eyes, muscles deep within your eyes, jaw, and back. Go to the muscles in your neck, the front of the neck, your shoulders, upper arms, lower arms, and hands. Now see the muscles at the top of your spine, down through the shoulder blades, the waist, and hips. Relax your stomach, thighs, legs, and feet.

Take this time to set your intention. Intend for it to be a time of renewal and exploration as you are guided to recover that which needs to be healed, to uncover your hidden gifts, talents, dreams, and passions, and to discover more fully that which is good, true, and beautiful in yourself. As you become more authentic, you become more whole and more able to share your good, true, and beautiful with the world.

Will you choose to be the *you* whom you were intended to be at the moment of your soul's very inception? Will you accept what God had in mind when you were breathed into being? Use your own free will now to align with heaven's will.

Set the intention to allow creation to be expressed through the unique vessel that is you.

Take some more deep breaths. As you read, allow your core self to reveal itself to you. Commit to be open, to learn and grow as you celebrate your uniqueness and your authentic self.

Life gives us so many opportunities to discover our authentic self. As you read this book with intense and honest contemplation and answer the questions at the end of each chapter, you will begin to discover who you truly are.

Questions for Reflection

Why is authenticity important to you?

In what areas of your life do you feel you are most authentic?

When do you feel you are least authentic?

Which people in your life do you feel are authentic and why?

Where do you find a lack of authenticity in your community?

Which people do you feel have been your most authentic role models?

Chapter 2

Discerning Truths

"You are one of a kind. Trust your own truth!"

— DEEPAK CHOPRA

To begin, it is necessary to examine two questions: What are your truths? and What do you actually believe? Our beliefs and patterns are two of the greatest stumbling blocks to authentic living.

Another miscarriage. I'd had another miscarriage. Would I ever be able to carry another child to term? What would I do if the answer was no?

So far, I believed I had done everything "right." Right according to what was outwardly expected. I had gone to college, gotten my degree, gotten married. My father believed a woman should only work outside the home if something bad happened to her husband. Otherwise, her job (i.e., my job) was to stay home and raise children.

I very much wanted children, but I also wanted a teaching career. I had simply assumed I would have children. Of course, without motherhood, who would I be? I also became very aware of my Catholic teachings and my father's beliefs. I wondered, *Are these my own thoughts?*

Eventually, I did have children. I feel deeply fortunate that I have two beautiful children who have grown into wonderful adults. I have six siblings, and all of us have children. I don't think any of us would have considered not having them, at least not as a choice. Our family and community's belief about having children was simply too strong. Facing a miscarriage helped me see the way cultural and family beliefs can become our unquestioned assumptions about life.

I'm sure you can think of areas in your own life where you took on the beliefs of your community and family without even realizing it. Your beliefs literally create your world. Often, these beliefs are unconscious and mysteriously lurk behind a conscious mind. You might even be shocked if you fully understood how much these beliefs have shaped your life experiences. Only by examining them are you able to cultivate an authentic life.

Careful study of this chapter on beliefs and truths can help you step into the fullness of the joy, purpose, and meaning of who you truly are. I attended Catholic schools where the nuns teaching our classes echoed the same beliefs I heard at church and at home. When I would ask the nuns, "Why?" I would always receive the same answer: "Just believe." When this answer didn't satisfy me, they told me I didn't have enough faith.

Somehow, this response only encouraged me to search for more answers that made sense to me. My questioning mind led me to Catholic teachers who did not agree with everything the Church was teaching. This encouraged me to search even further. I began a lifelong quest for something beyond dogma. In searching for truths that resonate with my own spirit, I have created a philosophy to live by that feels authentic to me. The search is not over. It continues to unfold every day, enhancing my life.

This is what I mean by authentic truth versus unquestioned beliefs or assumptions. You may take on your parents' beliefs without considering whether or not they fit you. Unquestioned beliefs can also come from many other sources such as teachers, religion, people in authority, TV and media, and the larger culture. You can even be influenced in utero by your mother's beliefs and emotions. Before birth, babies have an awareness of the mother's immediate environment and her feelings about the pregnancy.

Often you adopt your parents' beliefs and never consider whether you actually believe them or feel as if they are your own. The religion you are exposed to as a child often has a deep impact and can unconsciously influence accepting or rejecting your parents' religious beliefs. The beliefs and truths of your parents' religion can become your truths. But only when you have examined them and decided to embrace them for yourself can you call them your truths. Not until I was a college freshman at a Catholic girls' school did I begin examining what was true for me.

I have no interest in telling you what to adopt as your personal truth. Rather, I want to encourage you to persist in your quest to embody it. Do your best to stay open to new ideas, even those that seem strange at first. Question everything until you uncover the truth of each thing that resonates with you.

Think of early space exploration and witnessing a view of Earth as one whole sphere for the first time. Imagine actually seeing that connected nature of our world. It was only shortly after those first brave steps into outer space that it became commonplace to fly to another part of the country or across the globe. Eastern ideas mingled more and more with Western ones. With just a few images, we gained a new understanding of ourselves as one world in a way no words could ever have communicated.

This is how the quest for authentic truths unfold. As you search, you gain an ever-widening perspective on the world. In a single moment, the way you have always seen things can suddenly and radically shift. Does it make your previous beliefs invalid? That is only for you to decide. Now you simply have even more richness of experience to draw from.

For me, this search is always unfolding, and it enriches my life every single day. What I consider to be true today may no longer be a truth for me tomorrow. The only thing I know for certain is that what I know is so infinitesimally small compared to the great mysteries around me. Gaining wisdom and knowledge from these mysteries is an exciting, lifelong process.

Your willingness to have your ideas challenged by others is an excellent way to explore what you believe. Do you find yourself defensive about a certain belief? If so, it may be time to examine it or at least explore your attitude around it. I enjoy being questioned about what I believe. The challenge always strengthens my understanding and deepens my truth. If I can't answer a question or concern, I know I need to do some research to become stronger in that belief or to expand my thinking into a greater truth.

A key to developing authentic truths is curiosity. My world is a constant exploration. I live each day with the truths I embrace at that moment, knowing I can be shown some different truths at any moment. One of my core truths, however, is that I don't know everything about anything. I find great pleasure in discovery. I enjoy uncovering unconscious beliefs and examining them. Gratitude for a new insight keeps me engaged in the process.

My openness and willingness to grow and change is something I hope will continue until I am no longer on the planet. New awareness, knowledge, and growing wisdom will always be available if we look for it.

Many times, the pressures to conform keep you from examining your own beliefs. No one wants to feel ostracized, especially not by the people we care about most. Unconsciously, you carry a deep desire to receive approval from your mother and father or other primary caregivers. What if they won't approve of your truths? Sometimes, the stakes for examining beliefs can feel too high.

I know someone who was raised Southern Baptist. Everyone in her family held the same beliefs. She even went to a Southern Baptist University. When she began questioning the church's dogma during her college years, she had difficulty connecting with anyone willing to support her quest for authenticity. "In college, I almost had a nervous breakdown," she shared. "Once I left the church, I felt very alone for a long time. Nearly everyone I knew went to church, including my whole extended family. They were dead set on getting me to come back around to their way of seeing the world. It took me an entire decade to find my own footing again."

As your consciousness expands, what you know to be true does not necessarily resemble your childhood religion at all. It is not always a rejection of former beliefs, but rather a trending toward a much more expanded and unlimited belief. This type of growth can encourage a greater responsibility for your life and the world.

For many, the need to be right can overwhelm any desire to discover a deeper understanding of the world. In this environment, you can find yourself either constantly defending your beliefs, or simply, never stopping long enough to examine them. Sometimes in the process of examining beliefs, it's possible to get caught in the trap of rebelling against the beliefs you took on without developing authentic truths of your own. In this space, you simply take a position to stand against those things. But what do you stand for?

My Southern Baptist friend can attest to this situation. As she puts it, "I spent many years angry with the world." She refused to believe in God and even made fun of Jesus. In other words, she spent her energy rejecting her former beliefs. She was not in the awareness that she had not created authentic truths of her own. "Everywhere I looked, I saw a horrible, hopeless world." As she began to meet people who had a different perspective on who Jesus was and what his teaching meant, she began to recognize that her childhood religion had given her a limited perspective on spirituality. Practices like meditation changed her life once she realized these practices were not at all opposed to the work of Christ as she had been taught. In fact, she came to believe Jesus Christ had embodied the essence of all spiritual traditions. No longer was she angrily rejecting everything connected with the church she grew up in. Rather, she had expanded her original, unquestioned beliefs into authentic personal truths.

Adopting a personal truth looks very different from angrily resisting old beliefs. You may have to start from the place of rebellion, especially if you received strong programming about what you "should" believe. Eventually, though, authentic truths will lead you into greater connection with life. They affirm, rather than negate.

Perhaps you have examined your own beliefs and continue to do so. Consider that your identity can still pose a roadblock to the process. Without realizing it, you can identify strongly with an experience, social group, or lifestyle that causes you to trigger and cling to old beliefs. The ways you define yourself can provide a feeling of certainty and safety.

Do you identify strongly with your political party, for example? That could mean you never consider a perspective on current events that your party does not support. Maybe education in a particular career choice has caused you to adopt a belief that you "should" live your life a certain way, even if it doesn't really make you happy. What about your age? Examine whether you have taken on beliefs about what life should look like when you reach a specific age. In youth, you might judge yourself too harshly for not accomplishing more, sooner. In my own life, the time came when I needed to examine and discard the belief that I was "over the hill." My age has blessed me with the wisdom of experience. In my eighties, I am living a vibrant, interesting life that continues to be full of meaning.

Ingrained beliefs do not usually dissolve rapidly. These long-held beliefs have provided you with a foundation for many years. Exchanging one belief for another or even just expanding a belief can feel empty, strange, painful, and confusing. Many people are too apathetic or lazy to put effort into the process. Shifting takes awareness, patience, and practice. However, when you do shift, you emerge in an expanded place with access to a much greater knowing. From this new perspective, you can create a more productive and joy-filled life.

Often, we create an unconscious belief in response to the challenges we have faced. This kind of belief can run and ruin your life. It can pervade your thoughts. Yet you might not even realize it's there. Now is the time to release those invalid and limiting beliefs, beliefs that anchor you in the past, in past memories of limitation. Beliefs that make you think, *I can't possibly do that; what would people think? I could never learn to do that now; I am too old.* Limiting beliefs are like veils that prevent you from seeing the enormous possibilities life offers you.

An iceberg illustrates this concept well. If you've ever seen a picture of an iceberg that shows the ice not just above, but also below the water, then you know the vast majority of its mass lies under the ocean's surface. In fact, a whopping 90 percent exists under the waves and out of sight. Our mind functions the same way. Many experiences are not consciously remembered. The truth is your mind has not actually discarded them. Not only has it recorded these events, but it has built belief systems to make sense of them. This is especially true of those with a strong emotional charge such as economic views, philosophies, or political convictions.

Have you ever tried to change a behavior you simply could not? "I don't want to procrastinate ever again," you tell yourself when feeling the stress of rushing around at the last minute to finish a project for work. A few days later, you find yourself procrastinating again. Why? Perhaps you're under the influence of an unconscious belief. Such repetitive behaviors can often point to feelings and experiences you've buried—the ones that remain below your awareness and are driving your actions.

By recognizing that awareness is the key to freedom, you can liberate yourself from feeling like the prisoner of your own unconscious mind. For example, consider procrastination. This behavior, which you can't seem to change using your conscious choice, offers an important clue. Your procrastination could stem from something in your unconscious mind that you want to avoid facing or feeling. Instead of beating yourself up for procrastinating, use this clue to gain deeper awareness of your unconscious beliefs.

Do you notice yourself always avoiding a similar kind of project? If so, why does that project feel so difficult to face? Writer's block is a common form of procrastination. On the surface, a writer can say, "I just don't feel inspired. I don't have anything to say." But what lies beneath this reasoning?

Many writers learned in school not to trust their own ideas. "The teacher knows better than me" was one belief that may have been created. Maybe the person learned to keep quiet to stay safe. Consider, "What I have to say doesn't matter" as a belief-creating experience, even if those words are no longer conscious. Or perhaps, there are the beliefs so many of us have taken on like, "I'm not good enough" or "I have to do everything perfectly to be loved." Any of those beliefs could stop a writer, an artist, a musician, or someone initiating a project for work from expressing themselves freely. An unconscious negative belief overpowers the urge to create something new. Procrastination results.

A good way to identify some of the core, unconscious beliefs you hold is to examine messages you received in childhood. "You're just like me," a father might say to his daughter. "You can't get along with anyone." This father is unable to teach his daughter good social skills, given his own belief about himself. When she goes to school and has a conflict with a friend, she will remind herself, "I can't get along with anyone." Instead of looking for a better understanding of how to resolve the conflict, she will blame herself. Feeling defensive, she will resort to the behaviors she learned from her father. Then the conflict will get worse. Now she has more proof that she can't get along with anyone. In time, this negative feedback loop becomes "her truth."

Unconscious negative beliefs are always in play. To identify them, avoid any tendency you may have to judge what comes up. Write down any negative messages you remember hearing as a child. You might remember statements such as:

- You always have to set a good example.

- You can't do anything right.

- You are so clumsy.

- You'll never amount to anything.

- You're not as good as your brother/sister.

Take some time to reflect on the statements you wrote down. Are you still holding on to one or more of them? If so, you will notice that you repeat them in your thoughts as "I" statements.

Negative self-talk will manifest in unexpected ways. Some of your negative beliefs came from things people said directly or indirectly to you. Others you created in an effort to make sense of difficult situations, confusing feelings, or the confusing behaviors of other people. We all do it. This is how the mind operates. It wants to control what it cannot understand. Negative beliefs are the result. Many of our negative beliefs can seem like they happened by osmosis. Because we can't connect them with one particular event or experience, we feel like they have always been there.

To understand this phenomenon a little better, consider this study. Researchers taught male mice to fear the smell of cherry blossoms by putting small electric shocks through their feet while exposed to the scent. Just a few weeks later, they bred these mice with females. The mouse pups had never been exposed to the smell, yet when they caught their first whiff of it, they automatically became fearful and anxious. They had even been born with more neurons for detecting that specific smell and more brain space for them. This points to epigenetics, a branch of science that looks at the way our genes express themselves. In this case, the DNA of the first generation of male mice did not change. What did alter was the way those genes expressed themselves. This new expression of the genetic code then got passed down to future generations.

What does that mean for you? You will probably not be able to point to a specific moment when your own unconscious beliefs formed. In fact, you most likely received some of your beliefs through osmosis, so to speak. A traumatizing experience that got translated into a mental belief could have happened to an ancestor three generations before your birth, or even earlier. When it happened does not affect that you live with the belief now.

Where a belief came from in the past matters less than the awareness of it in the present moment. Without awareness, a belief will drive your behaviors in a way that leaves you feeling out of control. Often "Life just happens" becomes one's mantra. Consider a young boy who is frequently told by his father, "You will never be a success." The father has always struggled at succeeding in the world because he heard the same message. He is passing the belief along to his son. If that belief lodges in the boy's unconscious mind, he will sabotage himself in ways he can't understand. Maybe he will avoid studying even the subjects he likes. Maybe he will forget important appointments, no matter how many reminders he gives himself. Even though he is intelligent, he might skip class or fail tests. "Why do I keep failing?" he asks himself. "This is not what I want to create with my life."

The universe is mirroring back to him the negative belief he took on from his father. To shift this pattern, he must first become conscious of this deeply rooted belief. Then he must examine it to realize it isn't actually "the truth" about him. Rather, it's a mental construct, an idea. When he sees this, he can begin to unravel this belief from his sense of identity. "I am not a failure," he can remind himself. "I can succeed if I put my mind to it." The more energy he invests in this new belief, the more he will see changes in his life.

Life always mirrors your true beliefs back to you. Not the ones you claim to believe, but the ones in which you have actually invested your emotional energy. It doesn't matter whether you are conscious of them or even if they are totally untrue. The resulting beauty comes from the way it empowers you to become aware of negative beliefs and change them.

In what areas does your life reflect your negative beliefs? Pick one area where you struggle. For now, you don't need to know your beliefs about it. Instead, resolve to spend the next few days reflecting on how you experience that part of your life. If you procrastinate, watch yourself without any judgment the next time you find yourself procrastinating. Ask yourself:

- *What do I feel in my body?*

- *What thoughts do I notice repeating in my mind?*

At first, you may not have words for your beliefs. That's okay. Simply observe. When you uncover a negative belief, ask yourself if this belief is really true. While examining the belief, listen to your heart. What does the heart tell you about the message? You can also explore emotional triggers to uncover unconscious beliefs.

Consider this scenario: At work, one of your colleagues has a habit of saying, "Can't you do anything right?" Every time you hear him say this, even to another person, you become angry. How dare he treat people this way? However, the person at the desk next to you just shrugs. "Oh, that guy is nuts," is his only comment after noticing your reaction. This coworker is unaffected. In other words, a belief of yours caused you to feel emotionally triggered by an arrogant colleague. You take it personally because it matches the things your own father used to say to you as a child. You hear a voice in your head say, "I can't do anything right." This man, with his words, has touched a nerve. His actions show you a possible unconscious belief.

When situations become painful or challenging, they present an opportunity to observe your negative beliefs and shift them. Unconscious negative beliefs often drive us to overdo: overwork, overgive, overeat, etc. Underneath these behaviors lies the core belief, "I am not enough."

Unconscious beliefs like this one do not have to become your fate. You have the power to change them. This process starts with awareness. In Chapter 9: Healing the Wounds, I will go into greater depth on how to use that awareness for transformation. For now, recognize that expanded awareness, new knowledge, and wisdom are always available when you look for them. It is difficult to give up our certainties, our positions, our beliefs, and our expectations. They help to define us. They often contribute to the belief of who we think we are, and without them, we struggle to recognize our true identity.

If a newer way of perceiving life can enrich you and bring about even more expanded thinking about yourself or your life, it is worth investigating.

Many great philosophers and learned men have searched a lifetime for answers, and many died with their questions unanswered. Life teaches much if you simply pay attention and listen. Your awareness, your truths, and your knowingness are unique. Apple CEO Steve Jobs once said, "Your time is limited so don't waste it living someone else's life." Don't be trapped by dogma or living your life as a result of other people's thinking. Most importantly, have the courage to follow your heart and intuition. Know yourself at your deepest core, your essence. Be open, be curious, be humble and celebrate you and your journey.

Questions for Reflection

What fundamental principles do you live by?

What truths or beliefs do you still question, if any?

What is sacred to you?

Have you discarded any beliefs that were once meaningful to you? Explain.

List beliefs that have held you back or caused you to lose a part of yourself.

Has there been a time when the need to be right was more important to you than the truth?

What negative beliefs do you still need to examine to determine if they are still influencing your life?

What limiting beliefs are still operating and keeping you stuck?

Chapter 3

Uncovering Patterns

"Authenticity is more than speaking. Authenticity is also about doing. Every decision we make says something about who we are."

— SIMON SINEK

Now that you have examined the beliefs that keep you from living authentically, let's look at another aspect that keeps you from living your true self. Think about your relationships. Do you ever swallow what you want to say to make other people happy? Do you do things for other people from a selfless place, from service? Or are you doing things so they will want you or like you?

I went to a retreat to dive deep within myself. As the teacher spoke about the pattern of pleasing other people to gain approval, I stood face to face with a part of myself I had never fully acknowledged. I left in a reflective state of mind. Was pleasing other people really all that bad? As an empath,

I found it so easy to know what others wanted or needed from me. I took pleasure in fulfilling their desires. Over the years, this pattern had served me well, both in my work as a biofeedback therapist who could give clients just the right treatments, and as a mother and friend.

"But I have helped so many people," I argued with myself. "Surely that's not all bad." Of course, it wasn't. But it wasn't all good either. I often swallowed my own needs and desires to gain others' affections. I had gotten so good at pleasing others that I often did not know what I wanted myself. I would go out of my way for other people, sometimes at a cost to myself.

Over the years, I had seen this pattern play out in a negative way with some of my clients. Two parents came to me in desperation over their daughter's migraine headaches. The pain she lived with was making it nearly impossible for her to perform well in school or on standardized tests. I felt so bad for her that I did more than offer the recommended biofeedback sessions. I also gave her the keys to my office and trained her on the biofeedback equipment so she could come in on evenings and weekends to practice self-regulation and reinforce her ability to control and manage the headaches. I invested extra time and energy with this whole family. I went above and beyond the call of duty.

Unfortunately, the insurance check to pay for my services went straight to the family and not to me. Without even thinking twice, they spent it all on other things. When I brought up the subject of my unpaid treatment costs, they did not seem the least bit concerned about their financial obligation. They reluctantly agreed to give me small monthly payments to reimburse their debt.

I had overheard others say, "Ann is so nice," but I did not recognize the deeper implication of those words.... "Ann will never get mad, no matter what we do." I knew I was a pleaser and was often taken advantage of. I had believed it was a virtue worthy of developing, and I had a hard time recognizing the shadow side of this pattern and how it affected those around me. Unwittingly, I had locked myself into a way of being that prevented my authentic expression of myself. I became aware that my inner and outer worlds did not match. It was time to recognize that the pattern I had been holding so tightly no longer served me.

Fear and Patterns

Why had I taken on this pattern of pleasing others, even when it had negative effects on me and others I loved? Not surprisingly, it all began in childhood. But how? The most basic answer to this question is simple: fear.

As a child, I had felt afraid of losing the love and support of the authority figures in my life. Originally, the messages I heard from them awakened that fear. Perhaps you can relate. Maybe when you were a kid, you heard messages like, "Boys don't cry," or "Girls aren't good at science." All of us receive cultural messages like these, based on the era in which we grow up. A common social message when I was a kid was, "Children should be seen and not heard." Often, the messages you received from parents and other authority figures hit you even more directly. "Your brother is the smart one," your mother might have said in passing, or "You're too fat; better lose some weight."

Some childhood messages come in less obvious ways. If, for instance, your younger sister was born with an illness, you may have lost your parents' attention as they struggled to cope with the additional care they had to provide for her. Perhaps when you shared a problem, they responded by saying you should just be grateful you are healthy. Without saying it explicitly, they sent you the message that your needs had to take a backseat.

For adults, fear can take many forms:

- *The fear of not getting what you want:* a relationship, a job, a home, etc.

- *The fear of losing what you have:* through isolation, abandonment, financial ruin, or another's death.

- *The fear of not being able to control a situation:* often the result of vulnerability, criticism, and the unknown.

For children, fear takes the same shapes. Usually a child's fears focus on survival needs like love, attention, affection, and material needs like clothing, food, and shelter. Children are generally too young to provide these things for themselves, so they instinctively look to parents or caregivers.

As a child, to deal with your fears, those usually based on past messages and experiences, you had to convert incoming messages into beliefs about yourself. If you grew up with a disabled younger sister, you might have created a belief like, "My needs don't matter," or "I have to make myself small to be loved." Perhaps no one ever explicitly gave you any messages like this one, though most of us did receive at least a few destructive messages overtly. Either way, the real issue came from the way you interpreted and internalized the messages around you to form a belief about yourself. The more you practiced the belief, the more it became a part of your everyday operating system. Once it got woven into your day-to-day personality, it became what I call a concept. To overcome this concept, you developed a pattern of thinking and acting.

A belief like "I'm not good enough" is a concept that can drive your whole life. You may become obsessed with attaining perfection: perfect grades, perfect house, perfect kids. The childhood fear that your parents would not love you unless you performed well eventually drove you to practice behaviors you still rely on as an adult. Maybe you have no memory of anyone pushing you to succeed as a kid. Your parents might have even said things like, "We're proud of you no matter what grades you get." Still, along the way, you interpreted and internalized their actions, words, and body language, along with the input of teachers, ministers, and even other children, to mean you only deserve love if you do well in school.

More than likely, you interpreted at least some of the actions of adults around you in a way those adults never intended. This happens because of the wide gap between the brain states of childhood and the way adult brains operate. I suggest reading Dr. Joe Dispenza's book *Breaking the Habit of Being Yourself* if you are interested in more information on this subject.

If your mother had to leave you in daycare at a very young age because of financial pressures, you might have developed the belief, "I'm not lovable, and I can't trust the people I love to stick around." In truth, your mother loved you dearly. Your brain was still too undeveloped to understand this. Instead, you developed a fear of abandonment, one so primal you may not have been able to put it into words. It became a concept that still causes you to hold on tightly in close relationships. Ironically, this type of behavior has been known to push other people away, thereby reinforcing the concept that you are unlovable.

You can think of a concept as a self-fulfilling prophecy. The belief you form about yourself initiates a pattern of thinking and acting that eventually becomes a way of being. Through the Law of Attraction, this way of being draws situations to you that reinforce your negative belief and make a different version of life seem impossible. You make it a setpoint. Eventually, this setpoint feels so familiar that you believe it's who you are. Fortunately, the concepts you created about yourself and the patterns they inspire are not you. They are simply a collection of habitual thoughts and actions. Becoming authentic means shedding these habits. It means freeing yourself from the false "selves" that fear inspired you to create.

Practice: Uncover Your Patterns

Perhaps you already understand, at least intellectually, the notion of limiting beliefs, concepts, and patterns. Unfortunately, these patterns are often subconscious and not always easy to identify. My own life demonstrates this clearly. Even though I spent most of my adult life as a counselor and studied meditation and spirituality throughout that entire time, I was in my seventies before I could clearly see my own pattern of pleasing other people. I had probably overlooked my habit of pleasing others because I relied on it so heavily to navigate my life. Developing awareness and understanding of your core patterns takes time and practice. You can't simply think about the concept and expect something to happen. You have to observe yourself in action.

With this in mind, I invite you to *begin a two-week observation practice. Materials required:* a pen/pencil, a journal, and your awareness.

During this two-week period, once every waking hour, ask yourself: "*How am I feeling emotionally?*" and "*How do I feel physically?*"

(If necessary, set an hourly timer to remind you to consider these questions.)

Questions to Consider

- What are my thoughts at this moment?
- Am I tense? Where in my body is the tension? Why do I feel tense?

- Am I anxious? Why do I feel anxious? Where do I feel the anxiety?

- Am I bored?

- Do I feel happy? Sad? Joyful? Angry? Are my thoughts positive or negative?

- Am I obsessing about something?

- Where do I hang out emotionally most of the time?

Throughout the day, write down your findings in your journal. After several weeks, a single pattern or even multiple patterns may become clear.

Patterns of Inauthenticity

To help you make sense of your findings and to assist in the identification of your own inauthentic patterns, I am sharing a number of common patterns my clients and I have observed. As you spot some of them in your own life, remember to go easy on yourself. These patterns helped you survive your childhood. They have served you beautifully, and you are not bad or wrong for developing any of them.

The main purpose of exploring your patterns is to finally leave the past and its survival energies behind you, exactly where they belong. When you release a pattern, you can stop recreating that old manifestation and replace it with a future that feels better. Instead of letting old pain dominate your life, you convert your past negative experiences into a powerful source of wisdom.

As you observe your patterns, you might realize many of them match those you witnessed in your parents. Sometimes it can sting to recognize this. As a kid, you may have even vowed, "I will never (fill in the blank) the way my mother/father does." And bingo...one day you find yourself doing or saying that exact same thing you most hated and vowed never to do.

Again, you'll need to cut yourself some slack. As a child, you had a limited number of models. The people you spent the most time around, usually your parents, gave you the most input in terms of how to behave and think, and not just with words. In your brain, mirror neurons fired in sync with their verbal and nonverbal modeling. Your mirror neurons caused you to wince if you saw one of them (or someone else) bump their head or stub a toe, as though you could feel their pain in your own body. Mirror neurons also played a key role in your learning, both at home and at school, by helping you imitate others. As the old saying goes: "Monkey see, monkey do."

You might notice you have created the exact opposite patterns as those you saw in your parents. Maybe the vow you made—that one stating you would never end up like them—caused you to model your own behavior in opposition to what your mirror neurons reflected. As an adult, you might tell yourself, "I am nothing like my parents." You are, however, still locked into a cycle that arose from your relationship with them.

Keep in mind that you didn't have any control as a child over what your mirror neurons picked up on and what they did not. Mirror neurons fire more quickly than the neocortex, the part of the brain where you make rational choices and the specific area of activity not yet fully developed in childhood. Behavior patterns repeated around you likely got wired into your brain even before you could speak.

Luckily, you can rewire your brain. As an adult, since your neocortex is the brain's rational part and fully developed, you have much more capacity to choose which modeling you want to keep and which you'd like to ignore. As you practice new behaviors, you literally prune away the neurons in your brain that are holding onto old patterns, better known as habits. Breaking a habit might take determination, but it is not impossible.

As you reflect on the patterns presented, remember that many will appear in clusters. You might see that you have worked hard to please other people throughout your life, and you have also tried to accomplish this people-pleasing by trying to be perfect.

Manipulation

In our culture, most of us live in a sea of manipulation in the form of ads on television or propaganda on social media. We are constantly bombarded with other people's ideas, opinions, values, and feelings. When a store clerk gushes, "That outfit looks fantastic; you should definitely buy it," we instinctively know to take those words with a grain of salt.

Have you ever considered how often you impose your own opinions and ideas on your partner, friends, or kids?

Manipulation can be so subtle that you may not even notice you're doing it, or that someone else is doing it to you. It can look like you're being very nice. If you've practiced this one a lot, you know just how to sweet-talk another person into doing or saying what you want. On the surface, it seems harmless. But it keeps you from knowing yourself or relating to another person from the heart.

On the other hand, manipulation can be very overt. "Look at all the things I have done for you," a parent might say in an attempt to change an adult child's behavior. "You owe me." Children or others who have low self-esteem or feel powerless in their own sense of self are susceptible to implied and overt manipulation. Manipulation arises when the manipulator fears they will not get their needs met. Another way to think of it is as a fear of rejection. If we honestly ask for what we want or need, the fear exists that we might hear, "No," or that the other person will no longer accept us. If you experienced rejection of your wants and needs in childhood, then perhaps you learned to avoid additional rejection by using the back door, so to speak, and manipulating others.

Perfectionism

You might wonder what's wrong with trying to be perfect. Keep in mind that a pattern of perfectionism is very different from doing your best or achieving excellence.

Maybe you know someone who will not leave the house without perfect makeup, every hair in place, and wearing a cool outfit. Or maybe you're like my client, Betty, who would never think of inviting someone into her home until she had wiped away every speck of dust. A perfectionist is usually striving so hard to impress someone else that they do not express the real person they are inside. That inner self naturally excels in a number of ways that have nothing to do with perfect hair or a clean house. But the perfectionist has no energy left to get to know their inner beauty.

The pattern of perfectionism is truly a protection from criticism. It has nothing to do with excellence. Unfortunately, it actually forces you to live in an atmosphere of criticism all the time. You are constantly finding your own faults. However, in our society, perfectionism is often considered a wonderful quality. Unfortunately, true perfectionism comes from a lack of inner self-worth and a fear of being criticized. A perfectionist who is criticized will try even harder to be more perfect. This comes from the deep-seated belief that "I am not enough."

The Victim/Martyr

The victim and martyr are similar because each feels they have been taken advantage of in some way. Both of them often come from a place of low self- esteem and do not recognize their own value.

The victim seeks attention by having others feel sorry for them. Someone deeply mired in this pattern can create one tragedy after another, none of which appears to be their fault. They see themselves as the individual who is always affected by others' negative actions and never feels any sense of responsibility for how things have happened.

One unconscious way this pattern plays out is in how a victim relates to other people. Victims will often choose abusive friends or partners. A victim views life as a tragedy and is nurtured by others' sympathy. Being a victim is a very unhealthy way to get attention.

The martyr often has an exaggerated sense of responsibility to others as well as a deep-seated fear of abandonment. Martyrs will often take on too much responsibility for a project or situation and then complain that they have too much to do. Martyrs often have trouble setting limits and boundaries, and as a result, they feel taken advantage of by others, and many times, they are unaware of their part in the situation.

It is important to recognize that most of us fall into the victim/martyr mode from time to time. Do you ever find yourself complaining about what someone did to you without considering how your behavior might have helped cause the situation?

Addiction

You can be addicted to work, alcohol, drugs, food, sports, sex, shopping, etc., or any combination of them. Addiction can take endless forms. Yet it always points to the core pattern of avoidance. The addicted person doesn't want to face something buried deep within the psyche.

Most of us know someone who struggles with obvious addictions like alcohol or recreational drugs. We may not realize, however, how easily we can get addicted to things like television, social media, or even other people's advice. Anything you do repeatedly to avoid being with yourself can be an addiction. Addiction in any form kills authenticity. The addict runs from who they are to become someone they are not.

Judgment

Someone locked in the pattern of judgment always looks for and generally is able to find the negative in whatever is currently happening. It points to a lack of self-esteem or a feeling of inadequacy. Downgrading a person, place, or situation makes the person with this pattern feel better about themselves, at least for a moment. When that moment passes, the old feelings of inadequacy and discomfort return.

From time to time, most of us fall into the pattern of judgment. It is often said that what we see in others exists within ourselves. This is true for both the positive and the negative. Therefore, it is often helpful to ask yourself if what you judge in another is something you might want to look at in yourself. Someone who expresses judgment strongly can be hard to be around for any length of time. At some point, this person will surely criticize you, along with everything and everyone else. This pattern can be exhausting. Few people will admit to this pattern, and they are frequently totally unaware of their behavior.

Understand the difference between discernment and judgment. Judgment involves placing a negative opinion on another person, thing, or situation. Discernment is simply making a choice to see whatever one encounters with clarity. I choose apples instead of oranges, for example. I choose to go to this movie rather than that one. Or you might say, "I can see my neighbor is struggling in her relationship right now." You can see with clarity the foibles in another person without making a negative judgment about them. Two old sayings come to mind that perfectly sum this up: "There but for the grace of God go I" *and* "Never judge another man until you've walked a mile in his shoes." In other words, you can see someone isn't doing well without placing a negative judgment on them.

When we judge ourselves too harshly, we can unconsciously project that judgment outward onto other people. It feels less stressful, at least in the moment, to displace personal judgment onto someone else. Try going for a whole day without judging anything. Is it easy or hard?

The Rebel

In this book's context, a rebel is someone who has built an identity around rising up against someone, something, or some idea. The rebel uses their energy to "be against" whatever the moment seems to present. This antagonism can be expressed by a hatred of dress codes, resistance to authority on principle, or inattention to social rules for acceptable behavior. After all, "everyone" knows that limits and boundaries were made to be broken. For a rebel, opposition is an unconscious, knee-jerk reaction to life.

A rebel can list thousands of reasons why they don't like a situation, a person, a government, etc. However, this individual usually doesn't really know themselves. They rarely ask themselves if they hold any values worth standing up for apart from being a rebel. A rebel will happily stand against something without ever taking the time to consider how to stand for something in a positive way.

Along these lines, a rebel often has an overwhelming desire to be different; it's their way to be noticed. Most rebellion unconsciously aims at catching the attention of others. This stems from an early feeling of being invisible to others. As a youth, a young rebel frequently longs for but rarely receives any positive acknowledgment from parents, siblings, friends, or teachers, so they begin to explore ways to attract negative attention, believed to be better than no attention at all.

Self-Sabotage

"Oh, I am so sorry I showed up late for this meeting. My phone has an issue." "I can't believe I missed this appointment for the second time. I got into another car accident." These are common excuses you might hear when the pattern of self-sabotage is in play. Typically, someone dealing with this pattern genuinely desires to achieve a certain outcome, yet somehow finds too many obstacles along the way. Unconsciously, they create these obstacles.

Employing excuses is a common theme of self-sabotage. Over and over, a self-saboteur will let themselves down by failing to finish an important task, missing an appointment, or forgetting to do homework. Every single time, they come up with an excuse. Someone overwhelmed by this pattern has to manage so many excuses that the excuses themselves become the focal point. Their intended goal never seems to materialize.

Underneath this pattern lies a feeling of unworthiness. A person who sabotages their own goals doesn't really believe they deserve the results they desire.

Projection

Projection is the subconscious defense mechanism of denying internal feelings or urges you can't accept and, instead, attributing them to other people. You can project both the positive and negative aspects of yourself onto others. Here's an example: A married man feels strongly attracted to a younger woman at work.

Instead of accepting and working with these feelings in himself, he accuses the woman of flirting with him or he accuses his wife of infidelity.

Most of us can recognize at least some projection in our lives. Have you ever felt angry with a spouse or close friend in a way that seemed out of proportion to the situation? Maybe your spouse forgot to call to tell you they would be late coming home. When the time they usually pull into the driveway comes and goes, your fear for their safety eventually turns into looming anger. Unconsciously, you are projecting a memory of your father, a man who was an emotionally and physically distant traveling salesman. When your spouse finally arrives home, you dish out the same icy silence you used to give your father when he would return from one of his many trips. You don't see the generally thoughtful person you married; you only see your father.

Negative projection often leads to blaming. At this point, you attempt to make the anger from your past the other person's fault. This pattern becomes very difficult for the person who is receiving the projection because it usually has nothing to do with them. A person who projects also often has a pattern of denial. They are usually not aware or refuse to accept the qualities they attribute to someone else. This unawareness does not always relate to the past; it can also be very much in the present.

You can see how this pattern blocks authenticity. To stay connected with yourself authentically, you must find a way to connect with all aspects of yourself and your past—even the things you don't want to see or feel. It can be difficult to face these aspects, but with a persistence to uncover them, you will gain true freedom through the process.

Denial

A denial pattern often shows up in combination with others such as projection and abusive behavior. When you are in denial, you are choosing to see a situation differently than it actually is.

This coping mechanism can seem harmless. What's the harm in seeing the world through rose-colored glasses? But someone in denial will often overlook important signs that are obvious to anyone else. In denial, you can stay in unhealthy or abusive relationships, refusing to set boundaries merely by ignoring that you need any. The fantasy world you create in denial keeps you from living a life that's true to yourself.

The Pleaser

The pleaser wants everyone to be happy and doesn't want to disappoint anyone. They are often afraid to set boundaries because they do not want to lose a friend in the process. Pleasing others is a way for them to receive love; however, it is generally at a cost to them. The pleaser will often be very aware of others' needs and less aware of their own needs. Confrontation is usually very difficult and will be avoided at all times. A pleaser is frequently unaware of the shadow side of this pattern, thinking to themselves, "What could be wrong with making others happy?" If you are a pleaser, some difficult questions to ask yourself are, "Am I doing this to receive love?" *and* "Do I really want to do this particular activity, or am I just doing it because someone else wants me to?"

Hiding

If you have a strong pattern of hiding, you often agree with whatever another person says. In a group, you remain quiet. Picture the student who never raises their hand or the man at the back of the crowd. You are afraid of offering your own opinion or taking action because you fear you won't be accepted. Early in life, you decided, "Nothing I say matters anyway," "I am not important," and "I will be criticized."

In the pattern of hiding, you often hide the truth from other people. You only offer half-truths instead. Fitting in matters to you more than authentic sharing. The result is you end up feeling very alone, even in a group that has accepted the surface persona you created for them. Consequently, no one will really know you.

Passive-Aggressive Behavior

A person who becomes angry in the midst of many situations may display a passive-aggressive pattern if they never seem willing to discuss the underlying anger that causes them to be so upset. This behavior makes it very difficult and confusing for the people around them because the real issue is never brought up to be resolved.

The silent treatment is a classic example. If you give someone the silent treatment, they know you feel angry. By refusing to say something, you have sent that message. Yet that person may have no idea what actually sparked your anger. However, if they do know and you never reveal why you are angry, they have no clue how to improve the situation. Some other instances of passive-aggressive behavior include:

- "Talking trash" about someone with other friends without ever speaking your mind to that person.

- Making intentional mistakes or delays (that look unintentional) in fulfilling the person's requests of you.

- Having a hostile or sarcastic demeanor toward the person without openly explaining your feelings, or sulking.

If you are chronically passive-aggressive, then you probably also frequently complain that others don't appreciate you. Small slights become big drama to someone who often relies on this pattern because they are looking for reasons to complain.

The antidote to this pattern is assertiveness, or the ability to speak up for your needs and express your feelings clearly and directly. Note that assertiveness is not the same thing as aggression. With aggression, you bear ill will toward another person, even if packaged under a seemingly passive veneer. This aggression will hurt relationships. With assertiveness, you express your desires clearly, without anger or blame. You are not trying to force another person to do what you want; you are merely being open about what you want.

You can fall into a passive-aggressive pattern if you don't feel safe to express yourself honestly and vulnerably. Passive-aggressive behavior can feel like playing it safe. When you don't express yourself, there is a sense of avoiding rejection. Actually, you've only succeeded in projecting the self-rejection of your personal needs onto the other person. In the end, they will find it difficult ever to be close to you.

Understanding your moods and needs will always feel like a no-win guessing game.

Abuse

A pattern of abuse can take many forms: physical, emotional, verbal, or sexual. The person delivering abuse feels powerless and abuses others to gain a feeling of control or a sense of power over them. An abuser is often loud, angry, and/or sarcastic. This behavior can be the result of an unhealed family pattern where an abused child often becomes an abuser as an adult.

When you allow abuse, you empower this pattern. If you allow yourself to be abused, you may also find there is abuse in your family history. The difference is that you behave now as your abused parent did then. If you allow abuse into your life, over time you get good at numbing out the pain it causes.

Neither abuser nor abused feels good about being locked in this pattern. Often other kinds of abuse, like drug or alcohol addiction, accompany the pattern. People dealing with this pattern use addictions to distance themselves from the pain it causes.

On either side of this equation, you cannot express or know your true self. Many of the previous patterns could also have the component of abuse.

Moving Forward

I have briefly outlined some fairly common patterns. There are many others. The patterns previously discussed are merely a sampling of common patterns. When you find a pattern in yourself, explore your fear around it to identify the emotion's root. Ask yourself: What concept did I create to deal with my fears that has put this pattern in motion? Awareness is the essential first step in transforming a pattern. You may find it helpful to work with a therapist as you uncover your patterns. Sometimes awareness is all you need to shift a pattern in yourself. Another great resource is the book *The Inner Matrix* by Joey Klein. Read and then reread this book to help bring your patterns into awareness.

Questions for Reflection

What patterns are most prevalent in you? How do they keep you from being authentic?

Do you ever do something for others so they will think more highly of you? If so, ask, "Am I afraid that if I am present, without offering to do anything extra, I won't be liked?"

Out of fear of not being accepted, have you ever agreed with an idea, situation, etc., rather than voicing a different opinion?

Have you ever refused to face a situation because you couldn't accept what you knew was true?

Have you ever lied about a situation rather than owning up to what is truly going on, either in your own behavior or others' behaviors?

How many times a day do you judge another person, thing, or situation?

When in your life have you felt like a victim? With whom? How often?

Do you find yourself complaining about what other people have done to you?

Do you find yourself blaming others for your mistakes?

Have you ever been angry about a situation and displayed your anger but refused to discuss the problem?

Chapter 4

Honoring Courage, Honesty, Trust, and Vulnerability

"We need to give each other the space to grow, to be ourselves, to exercise our diversity. We need to give each other space so that we may give and receive such beautiful things as ideas, openness, dignity, joy, healing and inclusion."

— MAX DE PREE

Now that you see what can keep you from authenticity, let's explore the essential qualities for living an authentic life. These qualities include:

- Courage
- Vulnerability
- Honesty
- Trust
- Presence

- Judicious communication

- Honor and respect

- Limits and boundaries

- Vision and insight

In the next four chapters, I will examine all of them individually. Keep in mind that you can't always separate these qualities into distinct categories. Like threads in a tapestry, the qualities overlap. Themes repeat. Taken as a whole, they form a larger picture. By breaking down each quality individually, I aim to help you understand the concrete, practical ways you can develop this picture of your own authentic life.

As you read about each quality, think about yourself. Which of these qualities have you developed well? Which are underdeveloped in you? How could those weak spots relate to one of your unconscious patterns?

Authenticity is your natural state. All of the qualities we'll discuss in the following chapters are not things you have to learn. Rather, you will need to let go of the unhealthy patterns or negative beliefs you currently hold. Expressing authenticity works like tuning a radio to the desired channel. When you get yourself attuned to the frequencies of authenticity, you will not feel "fixed" or "changed," but rather, more and more like your real self.

Courage

"I learned that courage was not the absence of fear, but the triumph over it. The brave man is not he who does not feel afraid, but he who conquers that fear."

— NELSON MANDELA

When you think of courage, what comes to mind? Perhaps the courage of a New York firefighter rescuing people in the aftermath of the 9-11 attacks at great personal risk. Or maybe you consider the courage of a woman like Irena Sendler, who saved more than 2,500 Jewish children from the Nazis by smuggling them out of a Polish ghetto. And there's young Malala Yousafzai. She spoke out against the Taliban, whose members shot and nearly killed her at age fifteen, but were unable to silence her. She has won a Nobel Peace Prize for her international work to bring education to all women.

These tremendous feats of courage inspire us all. Yet you need not perform great acts like these to live a courageous life. It takes courage to live by your own design and courage to face your fears. Day-by-day and moment-by-moment, you will encounter quiet ways to express this quality in your life. Everyday courage may not make headlines. However, it can change the world. Consider the Me Too movement. Posting a personal story on social media may seem like a small act. On the other hand, it most certainly does take a strong dose of courage for women and men to share their stories of rape, incest, and sexual harassment in a public way. Each time someone posts their unheard story, more people gain the courage to do the same thing. Now we're seeing the impact of this movement on our whole culture. The courage of those who have shared their truth has made it clear: Sexual violence has affected all of us, and it is no longer acceptable to cover up or hide it.

Courage does not always come without a price. When you decide to live from courage, you may face isolation and criticism. Why? Not everyone around you will feel happy about the ways you may change. If you speak up about the things you have previously accepted, you will make others uncomfortable. Spouses, colleagues, friends—any or all of them can feel disoriented. You are no longer the person they've always known. What could that mean for them?

Still, in relationships without courage, love becomes dependency. Courage is the capacity to respectfully stand your ground, to say *NO*, even when the world wants you to say *yes*. This doesn't mean you won't feel afraid. Having courage means moving forward in the face of fear. It requires you not to step away from, *but toward* your fears and the fears of people around you. By doing so, you will transform those fears.

Sometimes you can feel afraid of positive things as well as negative ones. This has to do with our "safety zones." Unconsciously, we may become accustomed to a version of life that may not feel great, but it does feel safe. Consider the story of a young man who lost more than 100 pounds. He had a healthier body, yet he felt despair over the way women now treated him differently. They no longer opened up to him as a friend. He felt so uncomfortable with this change in his life that he put the weight back on. Perhaps his weight had given him a sense of safe invisibility. Being overweight had created a "comfort zone," both for him and possibly even the women in his life. So much so that he could not muster the courage to learn a new way of being. He held an emotional issue around his eating habits, not a physical one, as would be generally suspected.

I began this section detailing the quality of courage simply because you will need that basic understanding to embody all the other qualities of authenticity. Being more authentic requires you to change your patterns. Just like this young man, you will face unexpected challenges along the way. But, eventually, the pain of your wounds can become even greater than the fear of the unknown. Courage can take you to a place where you can deal with the roots of that pain so you can move past the pain to live as you truly are.

Practice: Breathing into Courage

A great starting place for making courage real in your life is to admit to yourself the times when you have been afraid. Do this without trying to ignore or deny how you feel. Only when we see our fears clearly can we invoke the courage we need to break their spell on us. Take a moment to do this now.

Some good news: You already have an excellent tool to help you face fear. It is your breath. Research shows that people who remain calm in the face of difficult circumstances breathe more than those of us who do not.

The following exercise is designed to maximize the power of your breath to help you remain calm as you work with fear:

- Start by breathing deeply. Close your eyes. For thirty seconds or more, do nothing but take deep, full breaths.

- Now think of at least one thing you know you're afraid of, one of your less pervasive fears. Are you afraid to speak in public? Scared of snakes? Heights? Do you feel afraid of forgetting something important at work or at home?

- Write it down. Do not censor yourself.

- Close your eyes again. Consider what you just wrote and breathe deeply.

- Now see yourself walking toward a situation in which that fear comes up for you and keep breathing. Allow your fear to rise and possibly intensify, but do not try to make it go away. Remember that courage comes in the face of fear. Simply let the fear wash over you. Be in the fear, but not overpowered by it.

- As you do this, picture yourself taking one small step toward that fearful situation, then one more. With each step, breathe deeply. Move as slowly as you need. Do not try to get rid of the fear. Simply see yourself moving toward the situation for as long as you can.

- Use your breath to help you become more comfortable with your fear. Once you've mastered this exercise, you can begin to work with deeper fears like being abandoned, rejected, or mocked. Use your breath to practice moving toward a situation where you feel that fear coming up.

Courage is an expression of integrity at its core. Courage is facing our fears, not running from them.

Questions for Reflection on Courage

When have you felt you displayed courage? Create a list.

In what areas do you wish to develop more courage?

Has there been a time when you did not display courage?

What does courage mean to you?

Honesty

"Honesty is more than not lying. It is truth telling, truth speaking, truth living and truth loving."

— JAMES E. FAUST

Authentic honesty involves much more than just telling the truth. It requires us to be straight with our needs, wants, and feelings. It continually pushes us to choose the higher road and act according to higher values.

Honesty with Yourself

For an authentic life, you absolutely must practice honesty with yourself. This can be easier said than done. Are you always honest with yourself about your feelings? Perhaps you think you are. Ask yourself if you have ever found yourself angry or upset at another person only to realize you're actually worried about something else, not the situation in front of you or the person at whom you're directing your anger.

In her course, *Rising Strong as a Spiritual Practice*, Brené Brown talks about reacting angrily to her daughter for not coming more prepared to a meeting they had scheduled to talk about her college entrance essays. The second Brené caught herself, she took a minute to step back and breathe; only then did she realize her daughter had done exactly what they had agreed to for the meeting. In reality, Brené was feeling upset and sad about her daughter leaving home. Her surface reaction of anger toward her daughter was hiding her deeper, painful feelings. When she got honest with herself, Brené could own her sadness. Only then could she admit to her daughter that her daughter had done nothing wrong.

As this example shows, a blocked expression of authenticity usually points to a deeper emotional wound. Perhaps you grew up in a household with an often-angry parent or a parent who didn't allow anyone to express anger. When you feel angry, you deny it—even to yourself. When your kids get angry, you deny it in them, too. Instead of trying to understand why they might feel angry, you send them to their rooms. By isolating them, you send the message that you don't want to know what might be beneath the anger or that anger is not okay. This may only make it worse.

Anger is just one of the feelings you might deny. How often do we say, "I'm fine," or "It's all good," when everything inside screams the opposite?

Our feelings offer us a way to know ourselves more deeply. It may not be appropriate for you to yell at your children, but being dishonest with yourself about feeling angry also doesn't work. When you practice honesty with yourself, you value your own internal experience—your feelings, needs, and desires—and tell yourself the truth about it as best you can.

Questions to Consider

- When have I rationalized my actions ("It wasn't my fault because..." or, "They made me do it," etc.) rather than face the truth?

- In what situations do I tend toward denial of my true thoughts, feelings, or actions?

- If I get curious, what do I notice about these patterns around self-honesty?

Another common lie is the lie of authority. With this lie, you hand your personal power over to an outside authority figure, someone who certainly must know better than you. Before you think you're above this one, consider the last time you saw a doctor. Did you trust their opinion, even if it directly contradicted your own intuition about your body?

We ignore our intuition frequently with trained professionals, from dentists to car mechanics. I am not suggesting you ignore their professional opinions. After all, you have consulted them for a reason; they have studied and gained experience in their chosen field. Consider, though, the wide range of professional opinions in any given arena. They can't all be right. If you stumble into the lie of authority, then you might miss the perspective that is right for you.

We often don't give ourselves credit for our own inner knowledge and wisdom but rather deflect to someone else. To get honest with yourself, begin to examine your self-talk. "I'm a failure" is often one of the hidden messages we send ourselves when we replay our mistakes over and over again. "I'm not good enough" or "I don't matter" are two more lies you may perpetuate internally. Plenty of others exist: "I'm a bad person," "I'm not lovable," "I'm a total failure," etc. All of these are lies. This kind of lie can be the hardest to stop telling. Why? Long ago, you made the lie a habit. As a child, you needed a story to make sense of the world around you. This storytelling does not point to weakness. Neuroscience tells us it's the way the brain functions. In a swirl of painful, negative, or disorienting emotions, the brain calms itself down by creating a story. It would rather make up a bad story than face a chaotic experience with no story at all.

Think of a young child who loses a parent suddenly. "It's all my fault," the child tells themselves. "If I hadn't been such a brat and made mom go to the store for me, she never would have died." From the outside, we can see that the story isn't true. The mother died because a drunk driver did not stop at an intersection and smashed into her car. If anyone bears responsibility, it would be the reckless driver. Yet this child could spend the rest of their life retelling the lie they created to make sense of this tragedy. They grow up constantly reminding themselves that they only hurt the people they love most. As an adult, they eventually marry. When the marriage fails, they remind themselves again that they only hurt the people they love. Ironically, this lie is exactly the reason the marriage faltered. They never opened up to their spouse. The spouse always felt very alone with them. As a result of often repeating a lie to themselves, they made that lie come true.

It's important to acknowledge that this kind of self-talk actually illustrates a lack of honesty. Compassion for yourself can help you see why you've committed yourself to a lie like "I'm not good enough." Once you recognize that your excuse is a lie, you free yourself to break out of the story's grip. Would you knowingly repeat a lie like, "You're not lovable," over and over to someone you care about? If not, why would you do it to yourself?

I encourage you to make being honest with yourself your top priority on the path to authenticity. Ultimately, the lies you tell yourself will directly affect the people around you. The person in the earlier example illustrates this clearly. Their lie to themselves profoundly affected their spouse and their relationship. Dishonesty with yourself will eventually express itself as dishonesty with others. There is no way around it.

Honesty with Others

Perhaps you grew up with a parent who taught you not to lie. Did you finish your homework? Did you clean your room? Did you study for that test? No cheating! We learned to think of lies as what we say to other people about our commitments and responsibilities. Can you tell a lie by failing to mention something? Perhaps you have told little white lies about your personal truth, for example; you lied about your feelings or experiences to please another.

The lack of honest communication might save you from discomfort in the short term. However, over the long haul, this pattern will eventually breed resentment. Why doesn't the other person consider your feelings or your ideas? Maybe they are unable to do so, or maybe you simply haven't helped them understand what you really need. Let your needs be known clearly; don't hold back or feel undeserving.

Of course, it takes courage to share your internal experience with another person, especially if you fear it won't be met with acceptance. In relationships without courage, love morphs into dependency. In fact, an authentic relationship requires you to draw on *all* the other qualities of authenticity: courage, vulnerability, honesty, trust, presence, judicious communication, honor and respect, limits and boundaries, and even vision and insight.

Honesty with others also has a link with integrity. Can other people count on what you say? Do you say what you mean and do what you say? If not, you may have a habit of saying what you believe someone wants to hear, even if you can't deliver it.

Relationship Patterns Connected with a Lack of Honesty

Passive-aggressive behavior: Do you stay silent and collude with others, even when it's not your truth? This is bound to rebound into subtle resentment over time. One form of passive-aggressive behavior is humor that deflects. Ever had a joke directed at you that didn't feel like a joke, only to have the person insist they were "just kidding"? Hiding negative feelings behind humor is a specific form of passive-aggressive behavior that lacks honesty.

Exaggeration: Got a big fish story? It may seem harmless, but exaggeration of the truth often points to a deeper issue such as insecurity.

Blaming: It's easier to point a finger than to be honest about vulnerable feelings or admit our mistakes.

Questions for Reflection on Honesty

With whom do you feel you are totally honest?

What lies have you either initiated or colluded in for the sake of being included?

Which pattern or patterns do you feel keep you from being totally honest?

Do you feel "white lies" are okay?

List the ways you feel you are not honest with yourself.

Vulnerability

"Vulnerability is not weakness. And that myth is profoundly dangerous. Vulnerability is the birthplace of innovation, creativity, and change."

— BRENÉ BROWN

Vulnerability equals weakness, right? At least our culture has taught us this. Rambo, Xena, Wonder Woman, and Superman are all examples of our pervasive cult of invincibility. A true hero always controls (and covers up) their emotions. At least that is what we are led to believe.

One of the leading experts on vulnerability, Brené Brown, teaches the opposite. Grounded in years of academically sound research, her work reframes vulnerability as one of the most accurate measures of courage we have. Instead of leading to failure, authentic vulnerability actually leads to success.

Brené Brown's life offers the perfect example of this. After teaching a group of executives about the importance of vulnerability in the workplace, she realized she should practice the message in her own life. She rewrote her TED talk. In the new version, she made herself vulnerable by sharing some of her own most shameful experiences, without trying to make herself look good. To get over the sense of rawness she felt afterwards, she told herself that at least hardly anyone would see the talk. It was just the TEDx Houston, after all.

Within days, her talk had gone viral with millions of hits. Why? Because other people could deeply relate to what she had to say. Her vulnerability made them feel connected, not just to her message, but also to her as a person.

Consider those superheroes I listed above. Every last one of them has had to face risk and uncertainty. In real life, no one achieves anything great without help from others. This is vulnerability. Vulnerability is our most accurate measure of courage. To feel is to be vulnerable. Many people will do anything not to show their emotions, especially their deepest feelings. Vulnerability is also about being honest, even when talking about the rawest of emotions.

Some of our most vulnerable times are during hardship, divorce, loss of a loved one, loss of a job, or loss of a pet. These situations can bring our sense of vulnerability to the surface, as can times of extreme joy like the birth of a child, a marriage, reuniting with a loved one, or other such times when our vulnerability may be more easily expressed.

As the oldest child with six siblings, I was often told, "You have to be the example." Being strong, being responsible, and doing what I was told all seemed to me to be the best way to be a good example as requested. Showing any form of vulnerability was totally off the table. What kind of example would that be showing my younger siblings?

I have found it difficult to share my vulnerabilities even though I have many. Allowing them to be expressed is especially difficult with my siblings.

Sometimes even the most independent, self-assured person can be perceived by others to live without a sense of vulnerability. However, I believe everyone has moments of uncertainty and emotional turmoil that cause them to feel vulnerable.

I have become aware of my own vulnerability in writing this book. What will people say? What will readers think? Have I shared too much of myself?

I can even think of other unpleasant scenarios that could result from my self- exposure as an author in putting a book out there for anyone to read.

Consider the words of Theodore Roosevelt:

> It is not the critic who counts; not the man who points out how the strong man stumbles, or where the doer of deeds could have done them better. The credit belongs to the man who is actually in the arena, whose face is marred by dust and sweat and blood; who strives valiantly; who errs, who comes short again and again, because there is no effort without error and shortcoming; but who does actually strive to do the deeds; who knows great enthusiasms, the great devotions; who spends himself in a worthy cause; who at the best knows in the end the triumph of high achievement, and who at the worst, if he fails, at least fails while daring greatly, so that his place shall never be with those cold and timid souls who neither know victory nor defeat.

Vulnerability in Relationships

Maybe you're someone who will do anything to avoid showing vulnerability to another person. More than likely, you also don't realize the ways you evade vulnerability. For most of us, vulnerability with other people feels counterintuitive. Dangerous, even. A bad idea. Inside, we all can sense the person we once were: the baby who could not survive without others, the child who needed approval from parents, the teenager who yearned for acceptance from peers. If you did not receive what you needed at any of these stages, then you probably decided to hide your authentic feelings and needs.

You will never live an authentic life as long as you hide. What's more, you will never experience authentic intimacy. For someone to know you, you must reveal not only the things you feel good about, but also the things that leave you feeling vulnerable. Your "weak spots." More than likely, other people already can see those weak spots more clearly than you realize. Whatever you do to cover up your "flaws" can sometimes push other people away. On the other hand, when you share your fears and shame from a place of vulnerability, not self-defense, you will bring other people closer. Think of Brené Brown's vulnerable TED Talk. It made her famous.

This doesn't mean you have to express your rawest, most vulnerable feelings with everyone, or even that you should. You've probably experienced someone who over-shares, also called floodlighting. You hardly know them, yet they freely share the blow-by-blow of their most recent breakup or relate painful stories from their childhood to you in detail. Social media plays host to lots of this over-sharing. Ironically, flood-lighting is another way to avoid authentic vulnerability. It's a performance designed to grab your attention, one without the intention to establish connection.

Your Response to Vulnerability

How do you respond to vulnerability in others? Your response can be the best gauge of your relationship to being vulner-able yourself. Does being around someone who reveals their vulnerable self make you uncomfortable? Maybe the person expresses their personal fear or sadness about an embarrass-ing or shameful experience. Do you want to quickly change the subject? Do you make a joke to lighten the conversation? Or maybe you jump in with a quick spiritual saying to cut them off, something like, "Well, it's all in divine order." If so, it's a sure bet you don't feel comfortable with your own vulnerability.

Perhaps you notice yourself feeling uncomfortable around someone who has just lost a loved one or is facing a serious illness. You may find that you fumble for something to say. You may even take action to avoid the person, which can leave the one who is suffering feeling even more alone. It is a common reaction to want to try to fix their suffering. There is no need for this. Regardless of how uncomfortable you may feel, often just being present is enough to let them know you care. The more comfortable you are with the vul-nerability in yourself, the easier it becomes to be present with others' vulnerability.

To avoid vulnerability, some choose drugs, alcohol, TV, computer games, perfectionism, etc. These are a few of the most common ways people distract themselves from their feelings. If you track your addictions, they will give you clues to your own comfort with vulnerability.

Questions for Reflection on Vulnerability

When or where have you experienced vulnerability?

Do you feel vulnerability is a weakness?

When have you resisted or refused to allow vulnerability?

What is your greatest fear around vulnerability?

Are you comfortable with another's vulnerability?

Trust

"Trust yourself. Create the kind of self that you will be happy to live with all your life. Make the most of yourself by fanning the tiny, inner sparks of possibility into flames of achievement."

— GOLDA MEIR

Trust calls you to live like a river, carried by the surprise of its own unfolding. To trust life, you must embrace the unknown and the unexpected. If you've had your trust broken, trust may not come naturally. Still, you can learn to trust with practice. As you move into a state of trust, you will find yourself letting go of attachments, beliefs, fears, and arrogance. These all arise from a desire for certainty. But certainty isn't real, so lean into trust.

The opposite of trust is trying to control the uncontrollable. A pattern of control can shut down creative expression. It causes you to fear a changing world—new technology, new ideas, and new frontiers in science and medicine. Without trust, you want to stop anything unpredictable, even if you can't.

Yet when you trust, you will no longer find the world around you overwhelming. Instead, you can enjoy the ride.

Trusting Yourself

Maybe you have had your trust broken by other people. That situation can make trust feel out of reach. The power within you, though, will never let you down. Leaning into it will lead you into greater trust.

Meditation is an excellent way to regain trust. The ability to sit in the state of a calm and quiet mind and connect with your heart is a true superpower. This is what meditation can help you achieve. Just as you would lift weights to build muscle, you can calm your mind and connect with your heart to build trust. The heart is clear, simple, and has no need to control. It sees with eyes of compassion. The more you connect with it from a place of neutrality, the more you train yourself to embrace each moment as it is. You come to see that every experience you attract is created to assist you in maintaining your forward momentum.

As you develop your ability to sit in silence, uncertainty loses any grip it may have on you. Clarity comes easily. Trust arises on its own, along with the answers you seek. Strengthening your trust in the power within allows you to experience a greater sense of security and feel less need to control. You will find that your mind devotes less time to making up those stories it creates when confronted with the unknown. You also won't get pulled as easily into others' drama. Creative answers arise freely from within. Your growing flexibility and objectivity make you more resilient. Life becomes more manageable.

Trusting our feelings often provides our truest and most immediate feedback. Our feelings signal important information faster than the brain. If we would only listen to and trust what our bodies are telling us, life would feel less bumpy. The gut responses are actually coming from the chemical reactions of neuropeptides found in the digestive tract. That is why we often sense a "gut feeling." The minute one walks into a room where there has been an argument or fight, our gut will convey a sense of knowing there is tension, anger, or frustration in that space. Many of us do not even notice what the body is telling us. It is important for each of us to acknowledge to ourselves what we are feeling. By not respecting what we feel, we often abandon the feeling and, thereby, abandon ourselves.

Trusting Others

Trusting another person means having total confidence in their integrity, ability, and good character. To trust also means to depend on or expect something with assurance from yourself or another. As with vulnerability, you should place your trust in those who have shown good reason for it. Perhaps you know you can count on one friend for a listening ear, but she doesn't do well with showing up on time. You probably wouldn't trust her with organizing an important event, but you do know you can call her when you're having a hard time.

In relationships, trust deepens with time and experience. The more we know another person, the more we understand their strengths and weaknesses and how deeply we can trust them. On the other hand, an attitude of mistrust leads to isolation. Did a coworker forget to finish an important project at deadline? If you approach them with an attitude of blame or accusation, you can easily damage the trust between you.

However, when you err on the side of trust, you come to uncertain situations with a curious mind. You leave the door open to increase your understanding and deepen your connection with the other person. Instead of saying, "You let me down. You didn't do your work," you start with, "I see you weren't able to meet this deadline. Are you able to share with me anything that is going on?"

This approach frees the other person to express themselves without defensiveness. Perhaps you'll receive an apology like, "I am so sorry. I got overwhelmed with everything I had to do for another project. I promise I will make sure you have it today." Or maybe you'll hear, "I learned in a meeting yesterday that our boss changed the deadline, but I totally forgot to tell you." If you hear this or something like it, you'll be relieved that you trusted the other person's good intentions instead of going on the attack.

The more you trust yourself, the more you will trust others, and when you can trust, life becomes much more free and joy-filled.

Questions for Reflection on Trust

Would you consider yourself to be a trustworthy person? Why?

Do you trust in the unexpected or do you want to control?

Are there areas in your life where you do not trust yourself or another? Does trust come naturally to you?

Is trust an issue for you? Why?

Now that we have an idea of these four qualities of courage, honesty, vulnerability, and trust, I invite you, if you have not already done so, to answer for yourself the questions following each quality. Examine whether you have fully developed each quality. If you find you are underdeveloped in any of them, address the pattern that prevents your authentic self from being realized.

Chapter 5

Realizing the Magic of
Judicious Communication

"You never know when a moment and a few sincere words can have an impact on a life."

— ZIG ZIGLAR

When you think of being an authentic communicator, does your mind jump directly to the notion of telling the truth? Judicious communication is a hallmark of an authentic life and involves so much more.

All communication grows from the way you communicate with yourself. In the last chapter, you had a chance to explore honesty in self-talk. Are the messages you repeat to yourself actually true? If not, then your self-talk is not authentic. You can get so used to the lies you tell yourself that you can't even spot them. How can you know if you're even telling yourself the truth?

Do you hear yourself using black and white language like "always" or "never"? For example, you might hear the voice in your head say, "I always make the same mistake," or "I am never going to get this right." This is a sure sign you're not telling yourself the truth. Strictly speaking, you can't "always" fail or "never" win, even with the worst odds. These words are clues that you're stuck in an emotional loop.

This looping underlies most of our misguided self-talk. You believe a thing about yourself and always notice evidence to support it. The evidence seems ironclad, especially since it reinforces your strong belief. This "loop" enables you to keep existing beliefs by not being open to receiving clues to dig deeper. It is reminiscent of a detective show where the head cop's primary incentive is to pronounce as quickly as possible, "Case closed."

What would happen, though, if you began to doubt the "solid case" your mind generated about you? Instead of looking for evidence of your faults, you could look for proof of what makes you wonderful. All of us, every last one of us, have both strengths and weaknesses. You always have a choice about whether you allow your strengths or weaknesses to grab your focus.

Does the evidence of the story you're telling yourself refer to earlier experiences, most likely painful ones? Perhaps you have wordless flashes of memory that support your story or you even hear yourself repeating phrases like, "My mother always told me I...." If your self-talk story's proof comes from the past, then it likely isn't truth. It's simply an identity you've gotten used to recreating over and over again for yourself—a habit of mind.

"I'm not lovable," a young woman tells herself, but how does she know this? For one thing, she's overweight. Everyone knows fat women don't get dates. That's obvious. She's not that pretty, either. Her dad would teasingly say she "had a great face for radio." He was also the one who took her to Weight Watchers, starting in the second grade.

She was also told she was too loud. As a kid, she was constantly asked to use her "inside voice." It didn't feel like she got anything right. She had no clue how to fit in. She'd always be the one with egg on her face, saying just the wrong thing at the wrong time. Her dad would reinforce her negative beliefs by saying, "You're just like me. You can't get along with anyone." Naturally, whenever she experienced an awkward social moment, she reminded herself, "I am hopeless. See? Of course, it's true that I am not lovable." Sigh....

Do you see in this self-talk monologue how often the word "always" appears? "Never" is there, too, along with other words that imply a similar meaning. There are phrases like, "You can't get along with anyone." There is a lot of "evidence" available to keep her mind busy skipping from one piece of it to the next, similar to a lawyer giving his closing arguments for a case.

This woman also continually referred back to messages she got in childhood during her negative self-talk sessions. The messages were old and had been a part of her awareness for so long that they felt true, even if they weren't. For many years, she quietly rehashed her negative stories before she began to see through the lies in them.

Are you building yourself up *or* reminding yourself of how bad and negative you are? Try changing your focus and begin giving yourself as many compliments as you can. Start witnessing the good that can manifest in your life as opposed to the negative.

Judicious communication with others reaches into every aspect of our lives. It includes a number of skills and attitudes. Listening lays the foundation for all judicious communication. In a conversation, do you spend more time thinking about what you will say next, *or* do you focus on what the other person has to say while they speak? Good listening springs from an attitude of presence. Attention lies at the heart of presence. To listen fully, you must pay attention not only to your own thoughts and feelings, but to the other person's as well.

Questions to Consider:
Assess Your Listening Habits

Do you notice yourself frequently interrupting others? How often?

Do you tend to speak more than others, either in one-on-one conversations or in a group?

Do you use a voice of authority or "The world according to..."?

Do you ask meaningful questions about the other's experience in the course of a conversation? Do you listen to their answers?

Do you keep your heart open when another person speaks?

Some of us are great talkers and some are great listeners. It takes both for a conversation to be meaningful and enjoyable.

Nonverbal Communication

Body language, tone, and other non-verbal cues also play a key role in judicious communication. You may have heard of the "seven-percent rule," the notion that only 7 percent of our communication comes from words we say.

Albert Mehrabian presented this idea in his book *Silent Messages*. He studied salespeople. How credible did their prospects believe them to be? Mehrabian reported that 55 percent of their credibility came from body language. Another 38 percent rose from their voice's tone and musicality. The actual words they used did not have a significantly noticeable influence on the people they hoped to influence.

Whether or not these numbers are always true, you must have your own intuitive sense that nonverbal cues play a huge role in effective communication. Take a phrase, any phrase, and play around with it.

"I'm so happy to see you!" a young child says joyfully to their new puppy as they wake it up with dog kisses. "I'm so happy to see you," a teenager says darkly, rolling their eyes at the harsh parent who has returned from a long time away. "I'm so happy to see you," a business-like attorney says with neutrality as they extend their hand toward an open chair to a client entering their office. You could imagine a hundred more scenarios where this same short sentence, "I'm so happy to see you," communicates something different.

Have you considered this aspect of your own communication? Think of a relationship where you struggle. Perhaps you can say you have never said anything negative to that person. But what kind of nonverbal signals do you send? Something as subtle as sitting with your arms crossed sends the message that you're not entirely open to what they have to say.

For many years, John Gottman, a research psychologist, studied what makes marriage work. Eventually, he came up with a very unusual way to do it. He details this work in his book *The Relationship Cure*. Instead of asking couples about their marriages, he created a one-of-a-kind lab where he could observe them. This lab was an apartment fitted with one-way mirrored glass and video-recording equipment. His team filled the lab with a succession of couples reporting many different levels of relationship satisfaction. The team taped and observed them all at length. At first, Gottman thought the team was doing nothing more than recording hours of junk footage. Even the happiest couples seemed to talk mostly about things like breakfast cereal and mortgage rates. Then he had a flash of insight. Each of those dull exchanges represented one thing: *a bid for connection*. Gottman realized the content of what a couple said to each other mattered much less than how each person responded to the other's bid for connection.

Gottman boiled his research down to three kinds of responses: *Turning toward, turning away,* or *turning against.* In each of these three forms of response, no words needed to be uttered.

- Turning toward another person can be as simple as looking up when a person enters the room or responding to a request with, "Yes, just as soon as I finish."

- Turning away can mean ignoring another person's question or responding with something like, "I'm trying to read right now."

- Turning against looks just as it sounds. It frequently demonstrates itself as arguing, glaring, and eye-rolling, along with more obvious things like yelling.

Once Gottman spotted these three responses, he was amazed to discover how much the small bids we make for connection, and how we respond to another person's bids, affect a relationship. Most of this happens nonverbally. In fact, a majority of responses to bids for connection come in the form of small gestures, facial expressions, attentiveness, and voice tone.

The couples who reported the highest level of satisfaction in their relationships had, on average, more than twenty "turning toward" bid-responses for every one negative "turning away" or "turning against." These "turning toward" bids could be as small and simple as a look or touch. But they added up to a reservoir of positive feelings to draw from during times of conflict. Couples can even develop a habit of

AUTHENTICITY AT YOUR BEST

turning toward one another that holds up during arguments. Instead of screaming, they might joke or play in the midst of their disagreement.

When Gottman's team began to apply this research to other relationships, they discovered these communication bids determine our relationship satisfaction in every area of life. Notably, most of this process happens beyond mere words. You can improve your feeling by improving how you respond to others' bids. Develop the habit of turning toward the others' bids. You may not agree with what your coworker is saying, but you could say, "Yes, I see your point. I understand where you're coming from. I wonder, have you considered this other aspect of the issue?" In other words, turning toward someone does not mean you have to ignore your own thoughts or feelings. You simply express your own perspective with consideration for the other person's experience. The same result can be achieved non-verbally, without saying a single word.

The effort you put into enhancing your listening skills and practicing positive nonverbal communication paves the way for healthy communication during times of conflict. Your positive communications with another person, even the small ones, register themselves in your relationship like deposits in a bank. Each one gives you more goodwill to draw from in difficult moments.

The "I" statement will also help tremendously. When communicating your anger or hurt, speak about it from an

"I perspective." Say, "*I felt* angry when you did that" rather than, "You made me so angry when you did that." Avoid using your words to point a finger at the other person. You can see that an "I" statement moves you out of blame mode. No longer is the other person responsible for your experience; you are. Of course, the trap you can fall into with the "I" statement tool is honoring the letter but not the spirit of the advice. If you say, loudly and through gritted teeth, "I felt angry when you did that!" then you are not likely to bridge the gap between yourself and the other person.

Using an "I" statement effectively requires real vulnerability. Much of this comes through non-verbal communication. You can say, "I felt angry when you did that," with the same energy of blame and rancor as the earlier, "You made me angry when you did that." The same statement, "I felt angry when you did that," can also be delivered from a place of softness as a way to acknowledge your own internal experience without insinuating an insult to another. Take it one step further by sharing your deeper feelings. Say, "I felt angry when you did that. I guess it just really hurt. Maybe it's not fair to you, but I felt like you were rejecting me."

Of course, a part of judicious communication is knowing when and with whom to share your inner experience this deeply. Always keep in mind that communication is a bid for connection. As you gain skill using vulnerable "I" statements, you'll learn that conflict can bring you closer to another person.

Here's a standard template for communicating about a sensitive topic:

- "When you said/did (X), the story I made up (what I told myself) was (X)."

- "When you said you didn't want to come with me, the story I made up was that you don't care about how hard it's been for me to deal with having my mom in the hospital."

The phrase, "The story I made up..." really helps you own your internal experience without insisting that it's true. We can thank Brené Brown for this effective approach to communicating from vulnerability.

Another important tool for judicious communication in times of conflict is active listening. It's easy to assume you understood someone if you heard the person's words. However, if you're upset, you're likely not to be fully present in the moment. Chances are you're busy (unconsciously) reliving an old upset. How likely are you to grasp the intention of another person's communication in that state?

When you find yourself upset by something another person said, you can say, "What I heard you say is _____. Is that right?" Often the other person will respond with a clarification that could change your feelings. If you sense that the other person is not understanding you, you can ask, "What did you hear me say?" Once you hear the way the other person took in your words, you may be able to clear things up with a bit more explanation. Be careful, though.

If, while attempting to clarify, you use words that make the other person wrong, e.g., "No, you never listen to me!", things could get worse. Instead, start your clarification with, "I understand why it sounded that way to you. What I want you to know is...."

Even with the best communication tools, you may still find yourself overwhelmed in an argument with strong emotions. Psychologists call this flooding. Chemicals and hormones—too powerful for you to override through will-power—flood your brain. Research shows that the only way to reset your nervous system is by taking a twenty-minute break. This helps your brain return to a more balanced state.

Timely Communication

Sometimes judicious communication means knowing when not to communicate. If you, the other person, or possibly both of you find yourselves yelling, banging doors, throwing things, or anything similar, then you have gotten to the point where you aren't likely to make any progress with your communication. In fact, you're more likely to cause harm if you continue. When the nervous system floods, you can say things you will later regret. This kind of communication can cause lasting damage.

In other words, choose the best moment, both time and place, to deliver your words. Consider a situation where a husband wants to tell his wife that he feels unhappy with his job and wants to try something new. The time to bring this up is not when she is walking out the door on her way to work. Also, the place to discuss sensitive matters would not be at a loud bar. With a sensitive topic, a poor choice of time and place can completely undermine your message.

Another aspect of timely communication is to share things in a timely way. What does this mean? Consider a situation where a friend says something to you that really hurts. Maybe you find it hard to say something to your friend in that moment about the way the words affected you. If you let too much time pass, however, you're likely to feel funny about bringing it up again. Still, resentment is boiling under the surface. You are likely to discuss your hurt feelings with countless other friends, desiring to reinforce your own perspective on the situation. All the while, you still haven't let the other person involved know that you felt hurt. Instead, your unresolved feelings could cause great damage to your relationship. Nothing about this is authentic.

Rather than remain quiet, clear the air with your friend as soon as possible. It is always best to do it in the moment of your upset if you can manage it. If you need some time for your feelings to cool, then make sure you don't let too much time pass. In most cases, a talk like this will improve the relationship if done using the shared tools. Communicating authentically about what took place will not hurt your relationship, as you may fear. You will come to understand each other much better, not just in this circumstance but in others. If you can't talk to your friend in this way, then perhaps your time would be better invested in friendships where you can.

Integrity in Your Communication

Are your words and actions in alignment? Alignment is key for authentic communication. Think of how bad it feels when someone promises something, then doesn't deliver.

A friend recently shared an experience she had in the early days of her marriage. Her husband had a close friend at the time who promised to provide the music for her fortieth birthday party. It was to be a dance party, and she had enthusiastically shared her own plans to do a lot of dancing with all her friends. Good music mattered. The party started at 6:00 p.m., but her husband's friend failed to show up until around 9:30. He hadn't bothered to set up any sound equipment in advance, so by the time he finally arrived, most of the guests had either already left or were leaving without hearing the wonderful dance music.

When your words and actions don't match, it can affect your relationships in ways you may not realize. "Say what you mean" and "Do what you say" are both paramount with this quality of judicious communication, and they greatly affect your authentic connection with others.

In modern life, we swim in a sea of electronic communication. Are you using these tools judiciously? For instance, have you ever caught yourself writing in a text, email, or post something you would never say to someone in person? We've all seen the vicious comments of trolls who attack people online with childish cruelty. It's far too easy to take out frustrations and insecurities on other people if you never have to see their faces.

It's also easy to fall into this sort of activity in a less-obvious way. Are you certain the text you just received was meant in the negative way you took it? Take a few extra seconds to reread the text. You might perceive its meaning differently. This is the electronic version of active listening. Another way to practice judicious electronic communication is to consider the way you use technology in the presence of real-life human beings. No one appreciates being ignored for a phone conversation, a text, an email, or anything else. This applies to family members and grocery store clerks alike. It is unlikely other people are interested in catching the details of your private life by hearing your end of a phone conversation or your music or videos at full volume in public spaces.

Here's a review of some of the negative patterns connected with undeveloped or underdeveloped judicious communication skills. Keep in mind that most of us express these patterns at some time. No judgment. Simply acknowledge the pattern, accept yourself where you are, and hold the intention to move through the pattern to a healthier form of communication.

- *Manipulation:* You communicate to get others to do what you want or to see you in a certain light.

- *Blaming others:* When you hear yourself say something like, "You made me..." or "You're the one who...", then you have probably caught yourself in this pattern.

- *Projection:* Projection often shows up together with blaming, but not always. If you have strong negative feelings and/or judgments about another person, chances are good that you're projecting your shadow self onto them.

- *Abuse:* All of these patterns are forms of abuse. In terms of judicious communication, the pattern of abuse can also take the form of name calling, insulting, or bullying another person with words.

Life creates magic when there is effective communication and life can be miserable with ineffective communication.

Questions for Reflection

In what circumstances do you experience the most difficulty communicating? Explain.

In what ways can you improve your communication skills?

Do you "say what you mean" and "do what you say"?

What signals does your body communicate to let you know to pay attention?

Whom do you find it most comfortable to communicate with? Why?

Are you as good a listener as you are a talker?

Do you "hold back" during a conversation? Could there be a pattern? Explain.

Chapter 6

Developing Awareness of Presence, Respect, and Boundaries

"Presence is not some exotic state that we need to search for or manufacture. In the simplest terms, it is the felt sense of wakefulness, openness, and tenderness that arises when we are fully here and now with our experience."

— TARA BRACH

Presence

Presence may seem illusive, yet as you becomes truly present to everything around you in any given moment, you realize just how much each moment has to give. Taking in all the sounds, smells, and feelings of your environment awakens you to a more expansive life and will open up a greater and more meaningful response to life.

The way we show up in any given moment relates directly to our authenticity. The past is already done, and the future never comes. Life happens right now: *Now*, and *Only Now*. Your presence arises in the present.

In her book, *The Top Five Regrets of the Dying*, palliative care nurse Bronnie Ware writes about her work caring for people in the last twelve weeks of their lives. One of the top regrets she heard from these people was, "I wish I hadn't worked so hard." It wasn't the work itself that inspired the regret. It was what people missed out on by spending so much time at work. What people grieve most for are the ordinary moments they never paid attention to. Being physically present alone won't create an authentic life. Intimacy only happens by being emotionally and mentally present while showing up physically. Attention is a key aspect of presence. Think of the dad who takes time off work to go to his son's ball game. While at the game, he spends the whole time on a business call. When his son makes a big play, he misses it. Will the son feel like his father actually showed up for him? His dad may have brought his body to the game, but his presence remained miles away.

Showing up and being present is important in a number of ways. Naturally, it is important to be clear and present when making important decisions. We can easily lose focus when not present. Consider how many of life's precious moments are missed simply by failing to be attentive in the moment.

In modern life, one of the most common barriers to presence is technology. Email, social media, TV, texts, etc., all pull us away from the present moment. How often do you see friends or couples in a restaurant engaged with their phones and not with each other? Part of the issue lies with brain chemistry. Smartphones and social media leverage the same addictive neuro-chemical channels as casinos and cocaine.

You get a hit of dopamine, a pleasure chemical, every time you have a positive social interaction. Smartphones offer opportunities for this all day long. While the hit of dopamine from a social media post may not equal the dopamine from cocaine, it still operates the same way. Dopamine tells the brain to reinforce the neural pathway that created the reward. At the same time, the brain thins out the number of its dopamine receptors. You will need more and more of the same stimuli for less and less of the chemical reward, even though your brain has not devoted much real estate to the activity.

Our technology also provides an excuse to limit our involvement with the outside world. Life is easy when one doesn't have to be vulnerable or present while remaining busy and distracted in our technical world. Technology does not allow us to be present with others in a soulful way. Being soulful is about listening and being present in the moment without the ego and personality interfering. The "to- do list" also distracts from presence. Does the rewarding desire to check things off your list keep you from the present moment? For one entire day, make presence your focus. And throughout the day, ask yourself these questions:

- *Am I here right now?*

- *If I'm not here, where am I?*

- *What percentage of me is here now and what percentage is somewhere else?*

When in conversation ask:

- *Do I watch the other person's facial expressions? Gestures?*

- *Do I ask appropriate questions of the other?*

- *Do I listen with interest and awareness without judgment?*

- *Do I interrupt or monopolize the conversation?*

Observing yourself, others, and your surroundings while being totally present can often bring you joy and make the world more available to you. The delightful smell after a spring rain, the crush of leaves underfoot in the fall, the way sunlight slants across your kitchen table—these are all small details that you might easily miss. Many artists say the reason they paint, write, or draw is it allows them to become more present with the world and themselves. In presence, the connection to your higher mind opens, offering insights, intuition, and perceptions that may not have been accessible to you before.

A good exercise for practicing presence is taking long, deep breaths. Be aware of the way air enters and leaves your nostrils. Notice your chest rise and fall. Feel your diaphragm move up and down in a rhythmic motion. Be present in your physical body. Can you feel your heartbeat? Your lungs fill with air? Your muscles relax? Your mind become clearer? Imagine how your perception of the world could change if presence were practiced regularly.

Questions for Reflection on Presence

What thoughts or activities keep you from being present?

What could you be avoiding by not being present?

Where do you mostly live...? Past? Present? Future? Why?

In what circumstances are you least present?

Respect

"Respect is one of the greatest expressions of love."

— MIGUEL ANGEL RUIZ

In a story from the Taoist tradition, the master Chuangtse is walking beside a river with a friend. "How delightful to see the way the fishes are enjoying themselves!" proclaims Chuangtse. His friend responds, "You're no fish. You can't know whether or not the fishes are enjoying themselves." Chuangtse replies, "You are not me. How do you know I do not know the fishes are enjoying themselves?" This funny story illustrates the reason respect plays an important role in an authentic life. Truly, you cannot know another person's internal experience. Through respect, you make room for it. In the process, your own world becomes enlarged; your life is enriched.

Think of respect as the active intention to reinspect or look again. Authentic respect is not simply a matter of taking off your hat during the national anthem or allowing another person to go ahead of you in a line. Rather, authentic respect requires you to consider new ideas and make space for different ways of operating. An open mind, like tilled soil, offers fertile ground for respect to take root.

Authentic respect doesn't end at having an open mind. It calls you to use that openness to understand and connect with people different from yourself. You can never know fully what experiences and ideas have shaped another person, even someone from your own family. How could you truly understand even some of these influences without investing time and attention?

Showing respect can feel like stretching. You may have to push up against the limits of your own truths or values. This can feel scary. You might fall into the trap of judging or resisting, the same way your joints can resist opening past their normal range of motion. Even the most "open-minded" people can fail at respect. Have you ever met a so-called "liberal" who looks down on anyone who does not share their political or religious beliefs? This person's mind may embrace new and different ideas, but their heart has closed down.

Authentic respect offers a powerful payoff: connection. In reality, we are connected with everyone and everything. This is the meaning of the teaching of Oneness, or Unity, so prevalent in most Eastern spiritual traditions. Yet without respect, you miss the experience of that connectedness. Judgment of others keeps you trapped in the lie of separateness. Regardless of whether you consciously realize it, this feeling of separation lies at the root of all your suffering.

Respect also gives you access to growth and discovery. New ideas keep life interesting. They help the brain stay agile. With authentic respect, you can discover new worlds, things, and people that nourish your soul. I read of a woman who first embarked on a career in anthropology in her eighties. Her respect for other cultures led her to realize, at this latter stage in her life, a passion for exploring them more fully. After a decade of study, she became a respected expert in her field.

Of course, authentic respect never means you have to adopt a new perspective if it does not resonate for you. It just gives you the awareness to allow others the space to hold their personal viewpoint without judgment or the need to control or change them.

Perhaps you find respect easy. Maybe it comes easily for you in some circumstances but is more challenging in others. If you believe you have no issues with respect, then one way to test your theory would be to explore a bigger challenge. Live in a foreign country, especially one with very different customs than your own. This exercise will surely cause you to stretch. It might also reveal where you've become set in your ways.

If you find you can't show authentic respect for another person, for a group of people, or in a particular situation, then you know you're up against one of your own emotional triggers. What does that person or circumstance remind you of from your own past? When you connect with your own emotional history from a place of compassion, you can regain your ability to show respect for others in any area where you previously found it hard to do.

Getting attached to your comfort zone can block authentic respect. If you always want things to be predictable, safe, or understood, then showing respect can be tough since it requires that you go beyond what you already know. To be fair, all of us like what's safe and predictable to a certain extent. Some people, however, like it a lot more than others. Respect can pose a big hurdle for this personality type.

Along these lines, you may tend to become more closed to new ideas as you age. Not everyone makes this mistake, but many do. The old saying "Age is just a number" means that your state of mind has everything to do with how well you will fare as you grow older. A rigid mind will eventually create a rigid body. Shut down respect for new ideas, new experiences, different cultures (including the cultures of younger generations) and life can be limited.

As you age, periodically ask yourself:

- *How resistant am I to new ideas?*

- *Would I rather be safe or grow?*

- *Do I find it hard to exchange a comfortable but limiting idea for a foreign (or scary) but liberating one?*

Questions for Reflection on Respect

When do you resist a new idea and why?

What does respect mean to you?

How do you respond to a different opinion than your own on a meaningful issue?

How does your body react when someone argues with you when they disagree?

Boundary Setting

"Daring to set boundaries is about having the courage to love ourselves even when we risk disappointing others."

— BRENÉ BROWN

Have you ever visited friends who ask guests to remove their shoes at the door? If you don't do this in your own house, you may have felt the ritual was a bit fussy. However, in spite of your personal opinion, you more than likely did it. You were entering another's home and showing your respect for their wishes. In their domain, you were expected to follow their rules.

Now imagine that you visited that same friend and, instead of taking off your shoes, they insisted you change all your clothes upon entering. Would you be nearly as willing to step in for a visit? Probably not. In the first scenario, you can honor another person's boundaries, even if it requires you to temporarily alter your own way of doing things. In the second instance, you decide your own personal boundaries need to take precedence over those of the other person.

With boundaries, no right or wrong exists. Most of the Asian world, for example, expects and even insists that people remove their shoes before entering a home. In the West, many people do not even think of it. Who is right? No one. Everyone. A good rule of thumb is the motto, "Do no harm." Beyond that, our personal boundaries are as unique as each one of us. No rule book exists to assist in navigating this territory.

Because there is no rule book, boundary setting can pose challenges for the best of us. If you had good modeling of healthy boundaries in childhood, then you are in the minority. More likely, you developed coping strategies instead of learning the skills required to set boundaries for yourself. So, what do good boundaries look like? Perhaps it's easier first to discuss what they don't look like.

Putting too many limits on others comes with a price tag. You keep people at a distance. Establishing inflexible boundaries, or setting up too many boundaries are both techniques used to create a sense of safety or as a guard against being used. Parents with extreme rigidity may find their children simply rebel. Sometimes rigid boundaries can even turn into bullying. When one intimidates others to get their way, they are no longer expressing authentic boundaries.

A person with too few boundaries can often fall into the victim or martyr role. The pleaser is often one whose boundaries are very underdeveloped or not developed at all. The pleaser wants everyone to be happy and content; it is very difficult for them to draw a personal boundary. They would rather make themselves unhappy or uncomfortable than restrict another in any way. Others frequently expect to be able to take advantage of a pleaser and, truth be told, they would be shocked if they ever encountered an expressed boundary from their target. As a result, the pleaser feels victimized.

Another aspect of boundaries is saying *yes* when one really wants to say *no*. We all know the person who always volunteers for whatever and then becomes overwhelmed and finds it difficult to say *no*. They then feel like a martyr. On the other hand, those who say *no* all the time might reflect on self-indulgence.

Children, as well as adults who are not familiar with boundaries, are often unaware of others' boundaries and also find it difficult to set boundaries of their own. Children who were spoiled, and mostly did their own thing or mostly got their own way, grew up having difficulty understanding others' needs, including their limits and boundaries. For children, healthy boundaries provide a sense of safety. A regular routine and clear communication of expectations and consequences are both good examples of limits that serve to help them thrive.

In the happy middle is someone with a healthy sense of respect. Deep respect for yourself inspires you to set clear boundaries with others. Respect for others' needs and limits helps you honor and even anticipate their boundaries and limits. You can begin developing healthy boundaries and limits at any time. Start by knowing yourself. Respecting others' boundaries does not mean you need to agree with or adopt them for yourself. Your own beliefs may be radically different. Yet when you honor another's boundaries, you remind yourself subconsciously that your own limits and boundaries deserve to be honored as well. By that same token, when you communicate your own boundaries, you are indirectly acknowledging others' boundaries as valid.

Our boundary styles have an intimate link with what we witnessed, learned, and deduced as kids. That's why each of us can have such unique blends of patterning in this area. If you struggle with setting boundaries, remind yourself that every time you turn down something you don't want, you are making more space in your life for the things you care about most. Without a clear *no*, you can never have a clear *yes*.

Brené Brown suggests this mantra: "I would rather have discomfort now than resentment later." In other words, it's better to have a few moments of the squirming discomfort of saying no to someone than to deal with the many hours (or longer) of resentment that will come from ignoring your own needs and priorities.

According to Bronnie Ware, author of *The Top Five Regrets of the Dying*, ignoring their own needs is one of those top five regrets of the dying. Over and over, she encountered people in the last weeks of their lives who had settled for keeping the peace with others instead of living the life they wanted. Bitterness and resentment, even illness, arose from this heavy regret.

Questions for Reflection on Boundaries

Under what circumstances do you have most difficulty setting boundaries?

Has a boundary of yours ever been ignored? How did you respond?

When is the desire to please others most likely to interfere with setting and maintaining your boundaries?

When are you most aware of others' boundaries?

List boundaries you have in your home, car, or workplace. Have you made others aware of them?

Chapter 7

Manifesting Vision and Encouraging Intuition

"It is this quality that calls us to remember our life purpose, our life dream. It is the relentless power within that extends an invitation to be who we are. It says to come forward to be our best selves."

— WAYNE DYER

So often we fall into our daily routines and habits and continue our lives as we have for years. We grow older and forget about our dreams and visions.

A question you might ask yourself is "What kind of world would I like for myself, my family, my community, and the world?" As we think outside the box and dream, we wonder, "How can I, with my gifts and talents, create such a world?" If we don't dream of something greater than what is, how can it ever occur? If our great inventors had never begun with a vision, the world would be in a very different place. Many of these inventions have greatly enhanced our daily life.

How are your gifts and talents being used to better mankind? Ask yourself, "How can I manifest and become all that I am and all that I want to be?" "Will my manifested self be of benefit to the world?" If you're not living a life of authentic vision, then start by making time in your daily life for reflection. Even those of us who regularly meditate or pray may not prioritize this essential ingredient to vision. Reflection takes time and attention. The more you invest in reflection, the more clearly your vision can emerge.

In time, reflection leads to clarity. To manifest something, you must begin with a clear picture of what you desire. Otherwise, it will never manifest. Say, for example, you decide you want to live in Hawaii one day. You visited one of its beautiful islands and you fell in love with the beaches, the waterfalls, and the culture. Later that same year, though, you see a special on TV about San Diego. Would that be a better place for you? You change your mind; you'd rather live in San Diego. That is, until you read about Bali. Maybe that's the best place for you. Are any of these visions likely to manifest? Not without greater clarity. You jump from idea to idea because you lack the necessary vision. Consider the deeper purpose of a move. What kind of life do you wish to create? How would a move support that vision?

Reflection is an integral step in the creation process. Remember that thoughts are actions. Yes, you read that right. Thoughts are actions. Consider that all your actions in the external world arise from your thoughts. Investing time for thoughtful reflection on your vision is like planting seeds in your garden. Some will bloom for a season. Others will never sprout. And some will lay down deep roots, bearing fruit year after year.

Many people hold over-sized expectations of what vision means. This short word, "vision," can conjure huge ideas, things like saving the world, becoming a famous musician, curing cancer, or inventing a revolutionary device like the light bulb or the iPhone. Know that manifesting such huge visions as these is not necessarily the goal for everyone. You don't even need to manifest your own visions all at once. Start small and you will be amazed by how your vision will expand.

My own work with this book illustrates what I mean. Initially, I created a workshop that expanded on the principles of living authentically. During that time, I was encouraged to write this book. Many felt it would be helpful and could enhance others' journey into authenticity in the same way they felt the workshop changed their lives.

This inspired me to write. I wanted to reach more people, offering the understanding and encouragement to live an authentic life. I observed a lack of authenticity around me and realized that few people understand the scope of what that means.

Who knows where my journey will take me next? I didn't write the curriculum or this book to become famous. I didn't even know how others would respond. Rather, I listened to the voice of vision within me, taking one step, then the next, and the next. No matter the outcome, I feel at peace with myself, knowing I have answered the call of vision within me.

Starting small often means starting where you are with what you already have or know. Do you dream of starting a new career? Maybe the thought of the required education and training stops you in your tracks. You would have to learn so much and make so many changes. Would it even be worth it?

The good news is you don't have to decide that right now. Instead, take one class on the topic or attend an evening lecture to get a better feel for it. Ask someone you know who works successfully in that field if they might consent to an interview or allow you to job-shadow. You could even begin by simply researching what training you would need, instead of assuming it would be too much. With any one of these small actions, you are already living a life of vision.

Many of us have heard about the power of intentions. Maybe you've even written some for yourself after reading the teachings of Louise Hay and others. You took action and came up with something in the present tense that you wanted to see change in your life. For example, "I am healthy, slender, and strong," or "I am wealthy, living in a home I love." You taped your written intention to the mirror as was advised. Maybe you even said it a hundred times a day.

Did it work? If not, then you probably missed two of the most important ingredients: *imagination* and *emotion*.

Consider the life of movie star Jim Carrey. He began in Hollywood as a starving artist. In that state, he wrote a paragraph-long intention of the life he wanted to live as a successful actor contributing to the world. He had a crystal-clear vision. But he didn't stop there. Every night, he would drive to Mulholland Drive, a wealthy part of the city. He would sit in his car, imagining himself living his intention with vivid detail. He visualized respected directors being interested in his work, and he even wrote himself a check for $10 million "for acting services rendered," giving himself five years to achieve it. All of these actions helped him imagine and feel himself fulfilling his vision.

In an interview with Oprah, Carrey once explained that he was doing these things to feel better. He would return home uplifted each night after this ritual and tell himself, "I do have these things; they're out there, but I just don't have a hold of them yet."

I don't need to tell you how well his vision manifested. He did, in fact, receive his first check for $10 million within the established timeframe for his movie *Dumb and Dumber*. His work in comedy made him a household name. In 2020, his net worth was quoted as being $180 million.

From Carrey's story, we can understand how intention works. The first step is to get clear on vision. Then use that vision to activate your imagination. See the outcome you desire actually happening. To create a manifestation, your visualizations need to be backed by uplifted emotion, a state where you truly believe you already have what you desire.

This ability to believe in what you cannot yet see with your eyes lies at the heart of vision. What you imagine must become vividly real to you. This only happens through the power of your imagination and your emotions. Both allow you to see and feel the experience in order to bring your intention into being. Picture all the benefits that will come, both to you and others, from the fulfillment of your vision. Experience how the joy of having your vision already manifested in your reality feels *right now*.

Many people give up on this process before it ever has a chance to work. Consider that Jim Carrey did it every night, during a time when he was completely broke. He had no evidence in his life to prove that any of it would come true. He simply set an intention to continue using this process to align himself daily with his vision until it became reality.

Vision without action is like seeds without soil. To bring its pure potential to life, vision must be grounded through deeds that are aligned with it. Many times, the actions you take help to activate the powerful positive emotion needed to bring your vision to life.

The story of Thomas Edison illustrates both vision and determination. Edison dealt with limitations, including a hearing loss from a childhood illness that would leave him almost deaf as an adult. Teachers labeled him as hyperactive and "difficult," so he only had twelve weeks of formal schooling. His natural inclination was to spend his time and money on experiments.

Edison's first invention, an electronic voting recorder, completely flopped. It worked fine, but he learned too late that Massachusetts' legislators weren't interested in a quicker way to record their votes.

Here, we can see what makes Edison so unique. Instead of giving up, he learned from this failure. His next invention, the Universal Stock Printer, was designed to carefully match business needs. He received $40,000 for the invention, which enabled him to devote himself to full-time inventing. Vision fueled his lifetime of prolific achievement. He received 1,093 US patents, and perhaps even more interesting, he filed 500–600 that were either unsuccessful or abandoned. In other words, at least half of his efforts were failures, but he never stopped taking action.

"I have not failed," he is famous for saying. "I've just found 10,000 ways that won't work." Bring this outlook to your action and you will find your own vision manifesting faster than you think.

What about us "normal people" who aren't going to invent the next big thing or lead a worldwide movement? Consider this example from the life of a friend. She wanted to be in a relationship, but she hadn't yet determined how to create a healthy one. Experience had taught her it would be hard to manifest a relationship; the whole idea felt overwhelming. Then one day she realized, "If I say I want a relationship, I have to do something about it." In that moment, she decided she would begin taking consistent action toward her vision.

She went dancing. She signed up for online dating services. She listened to and read everything she could on the topic of relationships. Then one night, when she was feeling particularly down, she decided to attend a free class being offered by a local relationship expert. His message lit a fire under her, and for the next six months, she attended his classes 2–3 times a week.

As "intentional focus" would have it, she felt inspired to attend a party held in the same location as her classes and noticed a man who immediately caught her eye. He was different from anyone she had ever dated. Nearly six years later, she reports they are still "happily together" and sharing a home.

Taking aligned action simply means doing what appears in front of you right now. As you act with clear intention, the next action will reveal itself. Then the next. Take action on what is presented to you every day and you will be brought closer to manifesting your vision in reality. Naturally, you may feel discouraged along the way. If you keep taking action, however, you can find yourself richly rewarded by a life that matches your vision.

Easy Manifesting Practice

Use this simple practice to make your vision a reality:

1. Place a picture of one thing you wish to manifest in a prominent place where you will see it often.

2. For three minutes in the morning and three minutes in the evening, look at the picture. (If three minutes feels like a long time, begin imagining all the ways this activity will benefit you, your family, and your friends while you are looking at the picture.)

3. Play some music that will help you feel the excitement and emotion of having this thing in your life.

4. Take any action that makes it feel more and more real to you. It could be research, looking at the thing you wish to purchase, talking to a professional regarding this desire, or any action that would enhance your thoughts about what you wish to manifest.

5. Examine your belief systems around what you want to manifest. If your belief system is not congruent with what you want to manifest, none of the above will work.

6. Be grateful and act *as if* it has *already* manifested.

NOTE: *Enthusiastically repeat each step daily until your desire is manifested.*

High-frequency emotions like faith, joy, trust, love, and courage function as food for your vision. Your positive feelings enhance your vision to assist its growth into reality. Observe your own thoughts and feelings around your vision. Do you doubt it can happen? Do you feel unworthy to receive it? Do you feel it will be a struggle to bring it about? Most of us carry negative beliefs that can hinder a life of vision. Become aware of yours. Coach yourself to make different thought choices when you catch yourself in doubt or discouragement. After all, thoughts are the first action you take in the process of manifesting.

Your emotional setpoint in your daily life also matters greatly for living from vision. When you think of an inspiring vision, don't you find yourself lifting your face upward? So, too, must your emotions stretch upwards. As a matter of habit, keep yourself as positively focused as you can, without suppressing anything within yourself that needs to move through you.

One excellent tool for keeping a high vibration is gratitude. Why? So many times, when you want to manifest a vision, you focus on what you don't have. Unwittingly, you activate a feeling of lack. The universe responds to your vibration. It agrees with your feelings of lack and sends you more of the same. When you actively cultivate gratitude for what you already have, you leave behind all feelings of lack. You activate a high frequency feeling of fullness and oneness with all of life. The universe can only send you more experiences to validate these feelings.

Most ancient indigenous cultures practiced gratitude as a way of life. One teacher, Julio Olalla, tells the story of meeting the last surviving member of the Ona tribe. Locals in Port Williams, on Navarino Island in Chile, called this man in his seventies "Granddad Felipe." Julio sought him out when he learned about him from others. He had so many questions for Granddad Felipe about how life had been in his tribe.

At first, one-word answers and small noises were all that Julio could coax from Granddad Felipe. As they walked along the shore, Julio asked questions and Granddad Felipe responded by simply nodding or shaking his head.

When they sat on the edge of an old dock to rest, the older man suddenly sprang to life. "How can those people just throw trash into the ocean like that?" he demanded, expressing outrage as he pointed at a cluster of people farther down the beach. "The ocean has given them so many gifts, so freely. Then they treat her like this. The Ona people always lived together with the ocean. The ocean was our father, our mother, and our life. We gave thanks to the ocean every single day for all of these gifts. I still do."

Granddad Felipe did not simply say thank you for a meal. In his tribe, he learned to practice gratitude throughout each day for things that most of us generally overlook or ignore. When was the last time you expressed deep gratitude for something as simple as the air you breathe or the soil that provides your food? More likely, you've put your energy toward something you want or need that you don't have. A wiser use of the same energy would have been to say "Thank you" to the earth for the gifts, freely given, from the air, the water, and the land. Imagine how an attitude of gratitude toward these simple gifts would transform an inner setpoint of lack into a stance of abundance. Pause and take notice of how much has already been received.

Another powerful way to work with gratitude is by perpetually dwelling in a state of thankfulness for your manifested vision before it manifests physically. Hold on to your gratitude while there is no evidence that your vision will manifest, choosing to stand strongly in the knowing that it already has.

Does this seem like a contradiction? It does only to the linear mind. The part of you with the power to manifest your vision functions outside of time. When you express your gratitude for the manifestation, even before you see it with your eyes, you align your personality with this nonlinear self. Soon enough, it will bring your vision to you in ways you never could have predicted.

Practically speaking, does it sound hard to do? Always remember that imagination plays a part. Remember Jim Carrey pretending he lived in that neighborhood he visited daily? He repeatedly told himself, "Everything I desire I already have, even if I don't yet have it in my hands."

Approach gratitude in the same way. Be grateful now for all the things that already exist in your future. "I'm so deeply grateful that these things are given to me," you can tell yourself. This way, you point your energy stream in the direction of the future where your vision is already manifested. It's now only a matter of time before it comes forth in your life.

Keep vision alive by fostering inspiration. This process is like building the soil in your garden. The more fertile your soil, the more easily your vision can take root and flourish.

"Inspiration...isn't reserved for high profile geniuses in the arts and sciences. It is inherent in our divine birthright. There is a voice in the universe inviting us to remember our purpose.... The voice whispers, shouts, and sings to us that this experience of living has meaning. That voice belongs to inspiration, which is within each of us."

— WAYNE DYER

Inspiration is your birthright. Every day it calls your name. You simply need to tune your ears to its voice. One way to do so is to take notice of the lives of people who inspire you. One example for me is Eleanor Roosevelt. She wrote "The International Bill of Human Rights," which recognized the inherent dignity and equality of all members of our human family.

Another person I am inspired by is Mahatma Gandhi. To me, his work for justice and social harmony through nonviolence embodies Spirit in action. Look for inspiration from people who have achieved something that matches your own current vision.

A friend of mine, who is actively working to heal her nervous system, listens daily to recordings by Dr. Joe Dispenza. At age twenty-three, Dr. Joe used his mind to heal a major spinal injury that doctors believed would leave him permanently crippled from the chest down. He now teaches about the power of the mind when used for manifesting. When she feels discouraged, my friend reminds herself, "If Joe did it, so can I."

You can also keep yourself inspired by surrounding yourself with people, ideas, and experiences that feed your vision. If you want to write a book, join a writer's group. Take a class in writing. Spend time with people who write. Make a simple commitment to spend ten minutes each day writing. Read Anne LaMotte's book *Bird by Bird*. It serves as a great inspiration on ways to help get your ideas onto the page. No need to do all of these, either. Just one could be enough to keep your inspiration alive. If one doesn't work, try another.

One key part of manifesting your vision requires doing nothing at all. Consider the garden metaphor once more. Anyone who has worked in a garden knows that hard work alone does not grow beautiful flowers or nourishing food. Sunlight, rain, and timing all play an essential part in the garden's success. Without them, your work with the soil, the seeds, or the weeds will yield nothing.

Can you make the sun shine? Can you make it rain? Not a chance. You do your part, but at a certain point, you have to step away from your garden and let the magic happen. Vision works the same way. Without your focused effort, your vision will never manifest. At a certain point, you must let go and allow it to come forth.

Have you ever struggled to find something to no avail? Maybe you misplaced your watch or keys. Maybe you couldn't think of the answer to a crossword clue, even though you felt you knew it. Finally, you gave up and went on with your business. Then lo and behold, you suddenly remembered where you had put your watch or keys, or the missing word flashed across your imagination.

This is exactly how manifesting works. The time comes when you must let go and allow your dream to find you. Many who write on manifesting emphasize how easy it is. Perhaps so, especially when you know how to focus your energy in a positive way on what you desire.

Authentic vision, however, calls for you to take your manifesting one step further. It means reaching for something you deem worthy. A vision arising from an authentic life should still stretch you. What do you want to see manifested in your community, your nation, and your world? How can you participate in that which will enliven and engage you? Surely you can do something to make life more rewarding for yourself and others.

To manifest this kind of vision, you will need to draw from all the other qualities of authenticity. It takes courage to have authentic vision. Courage to make choices that others may not support. Courage to face down your own fears and doubts. Without the quality of courage, you will surely stall in manifesting even your smaller dreams. When you pursue your vision, you will need the courage to step outside of your own comfort zone.

Trust is the partner of courage on this journey. You must train yourself to trust the voice of inspiration inside yourself. You have that voice for a reason. However, if you never trust it and you don't trust yourself, you will not be able to stand up to the storms of uncertainty bound to come your way on the path to a life of vision.

You will also need honesty. Honesty with yourself about your own strengths and weaknesses pairs with honesty with others about what you most desire from life. Without honesty, you can tell yourself you don't care about your vision, when in truth you are simply avoiding the work you know it will take to manifest.

With vulnerability, you will inspire support for your vision from other people. Only from a place of vulnerability can you say, "I need help." When you are not afraid to show vulnerability, you can multiply your own labors by enlisting help from people who love you.

Of course, judicious communication will keep the relationships within your support network healthy and strong. At every step of the way, your authentic vision will call for the ability to communicate well with others. Most authentic vision requires others' participation. Thus, the honor and respect you show others will return to you. Your own vision will receive honor and respect in turn. In the process, your own honor and respect for your vision will deepen as you see this reflection from the world around you.

Plenty of people won't automatically respect you or your vision. Some simply have their own agenda. Others might even oppose what you set out to create. Only when you set limits and boundaries can you protect your authentic vision from the indifference or criticism of others as well as give it the required nurturing. Vision thrives in an authentic life.

Questions to Consider

List your unfulfilled dreams.

What actions could you take to make a dream a reality?

If time or money were not an issue, what would you do with your life?

Explain what has kept you from taking action to make a dream a reality.

Describe the kind of world you wish for yourself, your family, and your community.

Honor Intuition and Insights

The Voice

There is a voice inside of you
That whispers all day long
'I feel that this is right for me
I know that this is wrong.'
No teacher, preacher, parent, friend
Or wise man can decide
What's right for you—just listen to
The voice that speaks inside.

— Shel Silverstein

This poem speaks volumes about our intuition. Intuition is our ever-present, inner knowing. It is my belief that intuition is often the way Spirit speaks to us.... We only need to listen. Intuition is the ability to understand something immediately without conscious reasoning. It gives us a knowing that we might never realize. Often, we are so busy or have so many distractions that we miss opportunities for awareness. Our intuition can reveal itself when we are calm and our mind is clear. At other times, it seems to come out of nowhere. It feels instinctual and can sometimes be that knowing or gut feeling when you walk into a situation or you meet someone for the first time.

One of my most memorable moments, in which my intuition was of utmost importance, requires the backdrop of the many tests I endured regarding infertility. The final test I faced required putting dye into my fallopian tubes. I was in the hospital and about to have the procedure done when I asked the nurse what would happen if I might already be pregnant. The question seemed to come out of the clear blue sky because I had had no signs of being pregnant at the time. She expressed her opinion that I shouldn't do the test if there was any possibility I might be pregnant. I somehow felt I should wait and do the test a month later. Only after making that choice did I discover I was pregnant with my first child.

Trusting your intuition is often so difficult. It is easy to second-guess or rationalize what your intuition might be telling you. As a practicing therapist, intuition was second nature to me when working with others; however, it was much more difficult to trust it when it applied to my life. I found that the more I trusted, the easier it became to recognize and take notice. I believe this quality can literally save our lives at any given moment. With awareness, openness, and willingness, the truth of this quality will become familiar to you.

Insights are thoughts or a knowingness that can come to you at any given time. They are often called epiphanies. An insight is usually a knowingness that comes when pondering a particular person, event, or experience. You might be concerned about how to handle a problem at work, but upon awakening the next morning, the answer is made available to you. When we are under stress, it is usually difficult to know what to do; however, sleep quiets the mind so the insights can surface and be known.

In essence, we need both our intuition and our logical mind to make the best choices for ourselves, our family, our business, etc. The conscious mind uses logic relentlessly. Our intuition and insights connect in a nonlinear way. They often defy conventional laws of time and space. Paying attention to these modes of knowing can result in a deeper understanding of your inner self. Deep inner guidance is always available and waiting to be realized.

One way to encourage intuition and insight is to write down thoughts and feelings that come from within. Do this in a calm place that allows your mind to quiet, and do not judge what becomes available to you. Don't betray yourself by ignoring this knowingness. Listen to yourself, your true being, and learn what your inside world has to say about the external.

Questions for Reflection

When have you found intuition helpful in making a decision?

Give an example of an insight that was meaningful to you.

How would you describe intuition in your life?

Have you experienced an epiphany at some time in your life that helped you understand yourself in a more profound way? Explain.

How can you better combine logic and intuition in making everyday decisions?

Chapter 8

Living Your Best Life:
Your Inner and Outer Worlds

"Authenticity is more than speaking.
Authenticity is also about doing."

— SIMON SINEK

I once took classes from a memorable yoga teacher. Almost immediately, I could tell she immensely enjoyed her work. She commented more than once on how much she loved her life.

When I learned more about her, I discovered she had spent years in business school—her parents' dream for her life. Eventually, she married a man also in business school. Then one day, she realized, rather suddenly, that she was not living her own life. She left both the business school and the marriage.

She had spent too many years pleasing her family with her choices. Now she didn't even know what she liked, much less what she wanted to pursue. To figure it out, she bought an apartment, moved in without furniture, and left the walls blank. Instead of filling the apartment up with her past, she wanted to discover what appealed to her as she walked through galleries and stores.

This move began her process of self-discovery. Freed from others' ideas and values, she was gradually able to uncover her own. Just as she had experimented with her apartment, she took that same successful approach to her career and, in time, she found that teaching yoga was her greatest passion.

This woman's story illustrates beautifully the principles of the Inner and Outer Worlds. Your inner world consists of your relationship with yourself: your dreams, passions, beliefs, feelings, likes and dislikes, and your identity. The love you cultivate toward yourself lays a solid foundation for having a healthy relationship to your inner world. Your outer world arises from your closest relationships, such as spouse, children, family, and friends. It also comes from your involvement with business associates, your neighborhood, your community, your city, your country, and the larger world.

Authenticity requires that your inner and outer worlds be congruous. Are you living in the outer world who you are on the inside by holding true to your beliefs, values, and deepest desires? Bridging the inner and outer worlds may not always be easy. You can see that my yoga teacher had to give up everything safe and familiar to live for a while in the uncomfortable void of not knowing. When she stuck with it, tremendous creative energy became available to her. In the end, she created a life she loved waking up to—one where the outside matched her inner being.

Relationship to Self

To establish a healthy inner world, you must make your own "love of self" paramount. The best friend you will ever have is yourself if you value and accept all that you are. But what is self-love? If you've never thought to cultivate it, the question can feel bewildering. Does it mean indulging your whims? Ignoring others' needs to exclusively pursue your own? Viewing your ideas as superior to those others hold?

Any one of these misinterpretations of the notion of self-love can arise for someone without a solid relationship with self. You might even fear you'll fall into one of these traps if you decide to pursue self-love. In fact, all of these behaviors arise from a lack of genuine love for self. Real self-love has many facets. One way to think of it is as the practice of holding yourself in delight and generous positive regard.

When you wake up, do you ask yourself, "What would bring me the most joy today?" The answer might surprise you if you pause to listen. As with my yoga teacher, self-love involves honoring your own talents, passions, and inclinations.

When you truly love yourself, you make space for self-discovery. What you truly desire becomes more important than impressing someone else. You let go of that age-old search for love in all the wrong places. Instead, you give that love to yourself. Many times, loving yourself can involve re-parenting a younger version of you that did not have your needs met. Self-love is dynamic and often involves many different considerations.

Louise Hay, in her book *You Can Heal Your Life*, gives many exercises for enhancing self-love. The mirror work she describes is an excellent tool to use when practicing self-love and beginning the process of loving yourself to a depth you may not know yet.

Start by storing up positive experiences of yourself. During the day, notice moments when you felt a spark of self-love, even just a glimmer. Maybe you did something you thought was admirable or interesting. It may have occurred during an interaction with another person or just something surfacing inside yourself, like a creative idea. It might be a time when you know you showed real character, even if others could not see it. Celebrate these moments!

Do not allow yourself to feel discouraged if you struggle with these exercises at first; simply stick with it and keep trying. You'll get there with enough practice. Your true nature is love. In time, self-love will emerge naturally from this essential core of your being as you put your focus on it.

Identity

How would you define yourself? Would your inclination be to offer a title like mother, doctor, athlete, or business owner? Or would you boast defining accolades, awards, and achievements? Some might define themselves by their ethics or truths, their compassion, their generosity, or their listening skills.

It's so very easy and relatively automatic to look outside yourself for identity instead of paying attention to what's going on inside yourself and who and how you are with you. Your sense of self remains constant when you build it from your inner world. When you look to the outer world, it will always fluctuate.

Elizabeth Gilbert does a great job explaining this in her book about creativity, *Big Magic*. She shares how she made a vow to honor her work as a writer. It didn't matter whether she ever became famous. It didn't even matter if she could make a living doing this work. She would remain steadfast in the pursuit of writing because she so deeply loved the work. Praise or criticism from other people would never get in the way of her dedication to the craft.

She remained true to her vow. At first, she simply practiced. She wrote dialogues the way her musician boyfriend played scales. She made sure every job she took also allowed the time necessary to work on her writing. Her work got stronger. Eventually, she was making a solid living sharing her words. Although many years passed before she became the famous author of *Eat, Pray, Love*, she had created an inner identity as a writer. She writes as a commitment to herself. To date, she has written eight books and many articles. Your true identity does not have a name. It is your unique expression of Source Energy. Only by cultivating your inner relationship with Source can you experience a stable sense of self in the outer world.

We previously discussed self-talk in Chapter 5. As you are probably more than aware, self-talk seems ever-present in our inner world. According to the Laboratory of Neuro-Imaging at the University of Southern California, we each have 48.6 thoughts per minute. That comes close to 3,000 thoughts per hour, and 70,000 per day. Phew! Imagine how many of these must be self-talk; thoughts that are messages *to* you, *about* you.

Do you talk to yourself like you're the most precious person you know? Sometimes self-talk is obvious. Whether silently or out loud, most of us have heard ourselves say something like, "You totally messed this up," or "Why do you keep making the same mistake?" Often, however, our self-talk is unconscious and remains just below the surface of our awareness.

Have you ever had a moment when you suddenly heard your internal voice because someone reflected it back to you? Perhaps you said, "I should not have done such a stupid thing," and the person you said it to kindly responded, "Don't be so hard on yourself. It's a pretty common mistake." Until that moment, you probably didn't even realize you had been criticizing yourself so harshly. Many negative self-talk habits take root in childhood. The critical voice of a parent, teacher, or sibling can easily be internalized by a young person.

In daily life, changing self-talk requires a personal commitment to take the required action. We can become so accustomed to our own negative self-talk that it may feel impossible to change. Fortunately, with love and determination, you can make significant headway in this area faster than you might think. Because most habits of negative self-talk arose in childhood, nurturing your inner child by offering some positive, heartfelt self-talk can be very helpful and necessary for many of us.

To help, here's an idea of what positive self-talk sounds like:

- *I'm right here. I will always be here with you.*

- *It's okay that you feel afraid right now.*

- *You did a great job today.*

- *I really like the way you do....*

- *This is a really tough situation. It's okay if you don't handle it perfectly.*

- *You can have all the time you need to learn.*

- *I will love you no matter what.*

- *I will be with you every day until you leave this planet.*

When you consciously initiate positive messages to yourself, you are creating a new internal environment. The little child in you suddenly feels safe. Now that child's dreams, talents, and potential are free to emerge naturally.

To live authentically, take on the practice of becoming more aware of your own self-talk. Even if you have understood this concept for years, you can always benefit from deepening this practice.

Feelings

A client once told me that only several hours after she left a party or event would she realize what she actually felt about what had happened there. She would find herself angry and resentful while thinking about the hurtful comments others had made and frustrated at herself for not speaking up about them.

Have you ever thought, "I should have said something. I would have reacted differently if I had only been more aware of what I was actually feeling"? Take a moment now to recognize that your feelings play a vital role in the creation of your inner world's landscape.

Are you always aware of what you feel? If you answered yes, without any hesitation, consider the possibility that you may not always be aware of your feelings. As a result of the subconscious mind's role in this arena, it would be nearly impossible to always be in touch with your feelings in any given moment. Have you ever caught yourself loudly and angrily saying, "I'm fine! I'm fine!"? This is one small example of a disconnect from your real feelings.

Feelings you disown, ignore, or deny do not go away. Think of them as the monsters in a horror movie, waiting for the perfect moment to come out of hiding. Begin to practice becoming more aware of what you feel inside. Through this endeavor, you will discover your inner self. To get the hang of it, frequently ask yourself easy questions like "How do I feel about this particular subject, situation, or experience?" Pause and take time for reflection. Keeping a journal really helps build a stronger awareness of how you feel.

Body Awareness

I have known two different men who recently died of prostate cancer. This form of cancer is very treatable when diagnosed early, but also very aggressive when ignored. Both of these men said, in very clear language, "I knew I had it a long time ago." One had even made a promise to his wife to visit a urologist when she expressed her concerns more than two years earlier. Needless to say, he broke that promise. As a result of their reluctance to seek help, the cancer in both of these men reached Stage IV before either sought medical attention.

Unfortunately, during the final months of their lives, both experienced excruciating pain that medication could not alleviate. Each of these men had worked professionally as a healer, focused on the physical ailments of others. When it came to their own bodies, they clearly were not listening. Think how much a daily dose of personal body awareness may have changed the outcome for either or both of them.

I share these stories without judgment. I offer them simply to advance your discernment. Your body constantly speaks to you through the language of sensation. Are you listening?

In modern life, most of us have learned to tune out the body's messages. Maybe your childhood church taught that the body is a source of temptation, sin, or evil. Perhaps you're like my two male friends, whose stoic Northern European cultures taught them that "real men" are strong and healthy. Maybe you got the message that your body wasn't good enough: too short, too tall, too fat, too skinny. Even someone who got the message they had a perfect body may have maintained a less than perfect relationship with it. By believing personal worth is connected to the way one's body looks, health is often sacrificed to look good.

In every moment, your body offers clues about your inner and outer worlds. If your heart is racing, you might be feeling anxious. If you sense tightness in your abdomen, perhaps your intuition is trying to tell you something about the world around you. Think of your body as a sacred reflecting pool. It reveals in your outer world the quality of your inner reality. A strong relationship with your body and its messages forms a solid foundation for a healthy and authentic life.

Gifts and Talents

If you are truly living authentically, it is impossible to ignore your gifts and talents. This can be as simple as sharing your warm smile or as grandiose as composing a symphony. Plenty of skills lie between these two ends of the spectrum. Most likely, you have many more talents and gifts than you realize. Have you been taught to downplay your talents and gifts so as not to be perceived as a braggart? Disowning your gifts is just as much an ego trap as being arrogant about them. False humility does not serve anyone. Only when you own your gifts fully can you give them freely.

Can you name, right now, at least five of your own talents or gifts? If not, ask people who know you to offer their assistance. This activity can spark new awareness of your strengths. Don't stop at five, though. Make an authentic relationship with as many of your talents and gifts as you possibly can.

Dreams and Passions

Without dreams, where would we be? Living in caves? Hunting and gathering all our food? Walking everywhere? A world without dreams is one without most of what we have invented, built, seen, filmed, or written about.

Faith is the engine of dreams. What you dream is invisible. It often flies in the face of what other people think is possible. Your faith in your dream, and in yourself to achieve it, is often the only thing that can convert your vision into reality.

Consider the story of Jeff Bezos. Imagine dreaming that everything could be available worldwide and shipped quickly. His vision must have sounded crazy. But instead of letting the world change his dream, his dream has changed the world. Amazon is a global success, and he is one of the richest men in the world. He accomplished what was once viewed as impossible.

Passion is the fire that fuels this kind of action. It's the burning desire that motivates you to do amazing things. When you feel passionate about a particular job, project, or experience, you put everything you have into it. When you finish the project, you might also feel your passion wane. In other words, passion is something to cultivate since it comes and goes based on your interests.

A loss of passion often underlies depression, sickness, and even death. The body's cells lose vibrancy with nothing to motivate, sparkle, or excite them. Without passion, life becomes stale. The will to live arises from the will to create, explore, and engage. The loss of passion is a major issue for our elder population. As people age and retire, many experience a lack of direction without the things they have always done. What do they have to live for?

Our culture doesn't help. We tend to hold our elders, who have immense wisdom and awareness to share, at a polite distance. In so many ways, we send them the message that they no longer have anything to give to the world. Too many elders believe this message. They fail to see the meaningful value of the contribution they have to make. Depression, loneliness, boredom, and other negative mental states result. They have lost their passion for life.

All of this can be alleviated in our culture by encouraging our elders to share from their lives. I know from experience that in my eighties, I still feel vital and not at all like the stereotypical "older person." Inside, I'm the same person I was in my thirties, except with far more insight and experience. For me, the life of Louise Hay exemplifies how any one of us can bloom as we age. She published her first book, *You Can Heal Your Life*, in her late fifties when her career was only getting started. It achieved worldwide renown and changed the way many people think about the relationship between illness and emotion.

You could say that Louise sparked and then fueled a whole movement in the world of publishing and in the lives of the people her company's work touched. Her publishing company, Hay House, has produced some of the finest metaphysical books, recordings, and workshops available anywhere. She accomplished all of this long after most Americans enter retirement and begin their decline. She remained active into her final years and left her body at the ripe age of ninety. Hers was truly a life lived with passion until the end.

Keeping your passion alive will keep you authentically engaged with your inner world and your own wellbeing.

Outer World Connection with Others

Your relationships range from your closest, most intimate connections to the person you casually brush past on the street, and every other encounter in between. Relationships with others are paramount, both in authentically expressing who you are and in becoming more aware of yourself. Realizing the vastness of self and bringing that unbounded joy, freedom, and expansion into daily life with others renews one's self and encourages others to do the same.

In every relationship, there exists three: two people, and the thread of the relationship itself, which links them together. That thread holds everything that each person has invested. Imagine all the kindness, caring, tenderness, and love, as well as all the anger, hatred, blame, or judgment.

Any energy you send toward the other person gets registered there. When you bring baggage from a past relationship into a new one, it also goes into that space. The health of any relationship depends entirely on how the two people involved tend to this living third entity.

This explains why being in relationship with others is one of the most rigorous practices on the planet. Communication can make or break a relationship, depending on its quality. Judicious, skillful communication is a must for an authentic relationship to root, grow, and thrive.

We choose our closest relationships for many different reasons. Some common ones include loneliness, fear, wanting children, money, sex, position, power, and wanting love. But if you truly know yourself, would you choose a relationship for one of these reasons? Unfortunately, none of them offer a solid foundation for an authentic connection.

Knowing yourself and being in touch with your own inner world takes time and energy. Fortunately, this investment will always pay off in the outer world of your relationships. When you create conscious relationships based on an authentic relationship with your inner world, then your outer world relationships can unlock a more authentic, caring, and confident expression of yourself. In any relationship, ask yourself: How does this connection bring out more of who I am naturally? If you do not get a clear answer, consider why. Use the outer relationship as a mirror of your inner self.

Outer World Connection to the World

In this era of immediate communication, we are on the verge of being swept away in the ever-expanding tide of what is happening throughout the world. The daily explosion of new information allows us to understand not only what is happening around us, but also what is happening inside our bodies and souls. Our collective perception of our planet and ourselves is currently undergoing a vast shift. We are here to establish a new and dynamic human society.

Can our global economy change from one of greed, scarcity, and abuse to one of abundance, peace, equality, and compassion? We need to challenge outdated, immoral, and unjust laws. Your awareness of what is happening in your own neighborhood, town, country, and planet not only enriches your life, but it presents an opportunity to share your authenticity to improve the lives of many. There are those who blindly accept whatever the media tells them, and there are those who maintain a healthy skepticism. There are those who allow themselves to be brainwashed, conditioned, and indoctrinated into living a fear-based lifestyle and those who gain the knowledge to remain ruthless with a courage-based lifestyle.

How can we become a beacon of courageous hope? We are interdependent beings on an interconnected planet. No place exists for passiveness in today's world. Nature is under attack. Our living planet is being destroyed by pollution all across the globe. Our lives are threatened by the pollution of air, water, and land. Technology can be of great benefit when used for good; however, we are seeing what can happen when self-interest supersedes global interest and technological advances are used in ways that ultimately destroy our health, our society, and our world.

We do our children, our grandchildren, and ourselves a vast disservice if we choose not to become aware and involved. In so many ways, we each can take responsibility for bringing the world we live in to a more kind, loving, and beautiful expression of itself. Every human has the inherent potential to be profoundly aware, conscious, and enlightened. To step into the fullness of who we are and consciously choose to live and share with others in that fullness is what authenticity is all about.

Questions for Reflection

How can you become more aware of the world in which you live?

What do you have to offer that will assist this planet in its evolution?

How aware are you of your innermost feelings? Explain.

List ways in which you can improve your closest relationships.

Describe the action steps you can take to improve your relationship with self, friends, and community.

Chapter 9

Healing the Wounds

"If you want to awaken all of humanity, then awaken all of yourself. If you want to eliminate all the suffering in the world, then eliminate all that is dark and negative in yourself. Truly, the greatest gift you have to give is that of your own transformation."

— LAO TZU

Healing. What does this word mean? The first dictionary definition reads, "to cure of disease." Now more than ever, we are living in a time of disease and disorder. Daily, we face massive pollution in our air, food, and water. Noise, chaos, dissonant EMF frequencies, and stress bombard us constantly. The body's immune system can only handle so much. Eventually, it gives way to illness, allergies, fatigue, and even potentially fatal conditions like cancer. For many, healing is the search for a cure to problems like these.

The dictionary gives another definition of healing, though: "To make sound or whole." In this paradigm, healing means more than curing physical ailments. It encompasses the emotional, mental, and spiritual dimensions of our being as well as the body. This broader scope gives us access to both greater physical health and lasting personal wellbeing.

Consider extensive research performed by Kelly A. Turner. She became fascinated with people who experienced radical remission from diseases like cancer. What had they done to beat their doctors' prognoses? Did they have anything in common? After years of in-depth study, she found that patients with radical remissions, despite the odds, did share some common factors. They all made radical changes in diet and added herbs or supplements. All of them did things like releasing suppressed emotions, decreasing negative emotions, finding a strong reason for living, embracing community support, and deepening their spiritual connection to life. In other words, physical changes alone were not enough to bring about lasting healing for those facing serious illness.

Even as we face more challenges in health in our modern world, we have access to more opportunities than ever before to create deep and abiding healing.

In my work with biofeedback, I have seen firsthand this kind of healing in my clients' lives. One of my most memorable clients was a woman with cancer. The cancer had spread throughout her body, and she had received many rounds of chemotherapy. When I began working with her, she spoke of how her husband and sons expected so much from her and seemed to take advantage of her sweet nature. As we worked together more, she started to learn about setting boundaries. For the first time, she began asking for what she needed from them, and eventually, she let them know how she felt about the way they treated her. They responded positively. They wanted to do anything they could to help her body heal from cancer. None of them had even realized they had been taking advantage of her.

After about six months of her embodying her new proactive personality, her physicians could no longer detect any cancer. Everyone was thrilled to hear about this miracle. Several years passed before I heard from her again. The cancer had returned. She readily admitted she had gone back to her old way of not speaking up for herself or setting boundaries with her husband and sons. I learned later that when she was transitioning, her husband did not want to let her go. She was very ill, and when he finally relented and told her she was free to leave, she died within two minutes. For me, this story powerfully illustrates the connection between our patterns, beliefs, and physical state of health.

Another example from my practice was a man whose neurologist had referred him to me for help with migraine headaches. This man was very successful in his career and happily married. In our work together, though, he had almost no interest in doing any of the exercises I used to help people control the dilation or constriction of the blood vessels that contribute to headaches. Instead, he wanted to talk with me about philosophy and the meaning of life. He devoured many of the books I recommended, and we had interesting discussions about them. Clearly, his soul wanted more from life. As he began to feel more comfortable with his yearning for a more meaningful life, his headaches were no longer a problem.

Just like my client, you may find yourself following a winding path when you enter the journey of healing. In reality, you are already sound and whole. Healing simply uncovers this truth. In her book *Start Where You Are*, Pema Chodron states:

> There is no need for self-improvement. All these trips that we lay on ourselves—the heavy-duty fearing that we're bad and hoping that we're good, the identities that we so dearly cling to, the rage, the jealousy and the addictions of all kinds—never touch our basic wealth. They are like clouds that temporarily block the sun. But all the time our warmth and brilliance are right here. This is who we really are. We are one blink of an eye away from being fully awake.

Healing happens in moments when you do wake up to the truth of these words. For many, healing may mean reaching into the depths of your soul and remembering who you truly are, your essence, your authentic self. Acknowledge the love you are as well as recognize where you have failed to acknowledge your inner life and why. What parts of yourself, your authentic self, are ready to be discovered or uncovered so that your life can be lived in the true expression of who you are? This type of healing will often heal the deepest of wounds. Without the knowledge of "you" today and the knowledge of what authenticity is all about, this type of healing would be foreign.

Following are fundamental principles I feel are essential to healing the whole person on all levels. Never has so much incredible knowledge, and so many healing modalities, medicines, therapists, and healers with amazing capacities been available to assist us in healing the body, mind, and soul. I would encourage you to seek what most resonates with you.

Awareness

Have you taken the time to answer the questions at the end of each of this book's earlier chapters? If so, you've taken the first and most important step in healing: awareness. As you become more aware of your own patterns and limiting beliefs, healing begins. Awareness empowers you to interrupt these patterns by "catching yourself in the act." Awareness provides you with the opportunity to replace them with the positive qualities we have explored.

Of course, this task is not easy. Be gentle with yourself. Know that you cannot change every pattern and belief in yourself at once, although if you're a perfectionist or a pleaser, you certainly might try! The work you do will certainly yield many results worth having in the form of a richer, fuller life. The more you make choices that reverse unhealthy habits, the easier these positive choices become.

Awareness of your physical body offers an excellent way to increase your overall awareness of yourself. The body constantly offers you feedback in the form of subtle (and some-times not-so-subtle) cues, which directly reflect how well you are practicing authenticity. Do you feel a gurgle in your stomach? A tightness in your shoulders? A sudden ache in your lower back? Notice that. What happened just before you experienced it? Often the body is speaking clearly; we simply need to take time to listen.

Daily meditation and journaling are excellent tools you can use any time to improve awareness in yourself. A book like Joey Klein's *Inner Matrix* is designed to help you uncover and journal about unconscious patterns within yourself. I have read this book three times and discovered something more about myself each time.

I continue to monitor myself daily, always following what I learned from this book. You will surely find a number of other ways to cultivate awareness. Awareness is the key that unlocks true healing by keeping authenticity at the fore-front of your choices and activities.

Giving and Receiving Love

Love is the strongest force in the universe. Pure, unconditional love can penetrate the density of all matter. The light that love brings is the supreme healer, for which there is no match.

Your cells thrive on love. They need it to survive. Every cell has a light all its own that it reflects to every other cell. The healthier the cell, the more light it can reflect. This is the essence of vitality. Pour love into every cell as you inten-tionally breathe love in and out. Allow your body to receive the love of God, the love of your angels, and the love of the people around you. Surrounding yourself with people who show love is very healing. Love is powerful. Use this power to empower you to heal yourself, to expand yourself, and to heal others.

You are love, and you can begin the healing process using the energy of unconditional love. Now you are opening your physical body to true health.

Expressing love to others is essential. Research has shown that one common regret people feel on their deathbeds is not having expressed more love. Fear of vulnerability or rejection can prevent us from sharing the love we feel.

Look for new ways to show love and awaken it in others. Simply validating another person can spark love. When you notice a particular quality in someone, appreciate the way they move when performing a small chore, or even enjoy the way they put an outfit together, that is a moment when you can express love. Say something. Let the person know you admire them. You can even acknowledge something you appreciate in someone you don't know. Offer a compliment on the stylish haircut of a person passing by. This, too, expresses love.

When you have developed a close relationship with someone, your expressions of love will naturally go deeper. However, they don't need to be more complex. When someone you love is hurting, the best thing you can offer is your presence. Listen. Ask questions. Offer your time and energy without trying to fix anything for them and your relationship will flourish through the power of love. For many, receiving this kind of love can feel uncomfortable or even unsafe. Pride or past rejections can keep you from opening fully to the love in your life. Simply allowing someone to comfort or support you in a time of need is an expression of love. By receiving love, you also give it.

Learn to surround yourself with people who outwardly express love, and become a person who does the same. This give and take will heal you. Gratitude will open you to a greater expression of love. If you don't feel gratitude, you can begin to cultivate it. Awaken that feeling within yourself through your own attention. Whether you are in one of the happiest or the most painful periods of your life, you can always uncover things to be grateful for. Keep a daily gratitude journal. This simple practice reduces negativity and frees your heart to express greater love.

In truth, you do not need to find love. You are love. This immense power, the strongest healing force in the universe, is your core self. It's your natural state of being. Bathe in this love. Allow the infinite love within you to empower and heal your personality. The greatest remorse is often love unexpressed.

Finding Joy and Meaning

Another important healing exercise is to find what brings joy and meaning to your life. Many people have no idea what brings them joy. In fact, some wonder, "What *is* joy?" It's easy to confuse joy with happiness. Buying a new car. Receiving an award. Starting a new dating relationship. All of these things can bring a rush of happiness. In time, however, this happiness fades. Of course, happiness is wonderful. It's good to understand, however, that it usually depends on something outside of yourself; thus, it comes and goes.

Joy, on the other hand, wells up from deep within you. It brings a sense of inner peace, contentment, and lasting pleasure. You might find that activities like running in the rain, playing with children, spending time with a special friend, being in nature, or painting a picture all spark joy. This high frequency emotion arises when you feel content, confident, connected, and stimulated.

For many, joy can be difficult to access. You may have learned as a child to "keep a lid on it." Adults can feel uncomfortable around the natural, easy joy of a child because of their own life experiences. Without realizing it, they do things to cut off the expression of joy in the children around them. If you grew up around adults who could not access joy, chances are good you don't give yourself permission to experience it either.

Ask yourself: When was I last challenged, surprised, inspired, touched, or moved? Often, a moment infused with one of these qualities is a moment of joy. Consciously recall each experience that comes up. This activity will help you access and activate joy in your life. Surround yourself with people who make you laugh—really laugh. Those who make you feel uplifted. These positive people can help your own self-image. People who can bring fun generally energize and enliven everyone's lives.

You also need to consider the negative influences you invite into your life; those that can shut down joy. Too much television news is a common one. News programs are actually designed to elicit feelings of upset, concern, and worry. Movies, too, can pull you away from an experience of joy, so choose carefully which ones you watch. If you prefer to watch media that brings you down, you may have unwittingly gotten used to a negative emotional state. Fortunately, you can flip that around and just as easily choose movies, TV shows, books, or podcasts that inspire you.

Positive influences, like people who make you laugh and uplifting movies, may not automatically awaken joy in you. They do, however, set the stage for you to access joy more easily in the future. Become aware of how your body feels when you spend time with positive people or situations.

Body Scan

- When you feel joy, where in your body does it register? Your chest? Your throat? Your head? Your belly?

- When you feel down or depressed, where in your body do you feel this? In the same places as joy? Somewhere different?

- Throughout the day, mentally scan your body. What are you feeling?

- Where do you feel it?

- What is the quality of the feeling? Perhaps hot, cold, smooth, choppy, clenched, open, bright, dark, or tight?

The habit of scanning your body will quickly build awareness. Use scanning to open new pathways to your own healing. Awareness is key! You cannot heal what you don't know or are unaware of. Stay present to strengthen your awareness of everything you think, see, feel, and do. You will be amazed by what you will learn about yourself.

What would you say was the most meaningful event that you have ever experienced? Sometimes it feels as if the meaning of life is so elusive that we are still continually looking for it. However, meaningful moments often are happening right now, in the present moment. You have heard the quote, "Life is not measured by the number of breaths we take, but by the moments that take our breath away." Those breathtaking moments would most likely be meaningful expressions of life. There is not one big cosmic meaning for all; there is only the meaning we each give to our life. What is meaningful for one might well be totally different for another. Finding your deeper meaning for life is as personal as you are individual. To help identify what is meaningful in your life, look for deeper meaning in your truths and values. What do you hold precious?

As you think and ponder what has meaning for you, incorporate those meaningful thoughts, ideas, and experiences into your life. Finding joy and meaning will enhance your environment and your health. Life has ups and downs, clarity and confusion, yet it holds a rich meaning that unfolds through living each day fully.

Forgiveness

*"The weak can never forgive. Forgiveness
is the attribute of the strong."*

— MAHATMA GANDHI

Forgiveness is such a challenge to the ego. It's easy to feel some version of the sentiment, "What that person did is unforgivable. Why should I forgive her?" I have heard clients say, "As long as I stay angry at that person, I won't get hurt." The problem? By staying angry, you are hurting yourself. Repeatedly reliving the wrongdoing of another continuously strengthens its neurological pathway in the brain. That pathway makes upset and pain easier to access.

Anger, resentment, and sadness, when mentally rehearsed and repeated, create a danger to your physical health. As you relive the negative experience, your physiology does too. Clearly, holding on to anger or hurt does not protect you from another person. Instead, it connects you with the person you cannot forgive, establishing a stronger negative connection than before. You also become more likely to repeat the same experience with another person since you've trained your brain to watch for it. You may have heard the statement, "Withholding forgiveness is like drinking poison and expecting the other to die." Contentment becomes elusive.

Forgiveness releases you and your body from this burden. Of course, forgiveness is not easy. It takes practice. Yet the positive impact it will have on your life makes the effort deeply worthwhile. Forgiving someone has nothing to do with condoning another person's actions, and it has everything to do with your own healing. True forgiveness may not impact the person who has hurt you, but it will most certainly free you. It is a gift you give to yourself.

The work of forgiveness happens internally. If you struggle to forgive someone else, you may be unconsciously having a hard time forgiving yourself. You could be angry with yourself for allowing the situation to happen. Maybe you tell yourself you should have done something differently or should have acted in a way that could have stopped the situation.

In *The Inner Matrix*, Joey Klein suggests that any emotion will dissipate if it is felt strongly for ninety seconds. Notice the feelings you have in your body when you think about the incident.... Anger? Hurt? If you feel the feeling, and only the feeling itself (e.g., anger, hurt) *without* the story for ninety seconds, the harmful emotions will dissipate and the act of forgiveness will begin. The process may need to be repeated several times before you notice the emotion's neurological impact changing as well. Asking for forgiveness from others and offering an apology are very helpful because they allow space for reconciliation to happen and for love to have an opportunity to be liberated or expressed.

One of the best ways to cultivate an attitude of forgiveness is to adopt this motto: Everyone is doing the best they can, including me. But what if you believe everyone is not doing the best they can? People can do so much better. "I could have done so much better in this past situation," you insist.

Is that true, though? Surely you acted as well as you could have, given your emotional state, your level of awareness at the time, and your cognitive understanding. You've heard the old saying about hindsight. You only understand what you did wrong once you've gained more awareness. If you had known better at the time, certainly you would have done better. If this sounds like letting yourself and other people off the hook, that's because it is. You get to release the past. Your love and understanding sets you free. From this viewpoint, you have a better chance of making a better choice in the future.

To be clear, you do not have to continue a relationship with someone who has hurt you deeply and is likely to continue doing so. Forgiving someone is different from maintaining a relationship with them. You can use good judgment to set healthy boundaries, which arise from self-respect, and still hold in your heart the intention of loving forgiveness toward someone. The act of forgiveness may be one of the most difficult experiences we encounter, but it is also one of the greatest acts that goes beyond superficial change and results in true peace.

Wholehearted Living

Wholehearted living is using every day as an expression of who you are. Whether at work or at play, you can embrace your life with zest and passion.

A few elements can help you live life to the fullest. Choose to have faith in either the Divine or something greater than yourself and nurture that belief with prayer, meditation, ritual, or whatever enhances and strengthens that belief. Believing a purpose exists for being here on earth as a human opens us to our great potential for high levels of consciousness and the ability to create beyond our wildest dreams. A life devoted to this greater being, perhaps known personally as God, Self, Source, etc., is a life of authenticity and freedom.

Another key is to make time for play and relaxation. Our culture values productivity and materialism above all. Yet without the rejuvenation that downtime provides, you likely won't be able to give yourself fully to your work. Without play, how will you access joy? By making space in your life to connect with others and have fun, you keep yourself connected with life itself.

I also suggest you eat as healthily as possible. Diets abound. The right foods for you may not be the right ones for another person. But a great starting place is to choose fresh, organic foods, the less processed the better, with little or no sugar. Considering the amount of pollution in our world, I also suggest drinking filtered water. Experiment to find the foods and water that bring the most vitality to your own body. Only with a healthy body can you experience life wholeheartedly.

As a biofeedback therapist, I feel dealing with stress in a healthy way is another important factor to wholehearted living. Healthy stress reduction can be accomplished with meditation, massage, and exercise, just to name a few methods. Depending upon your personal preferences, consider incorporating music, laughter, dance, and song to facilitate a more robust wellbeing as well. Wholehearted living will help you have clarity regarding your strengths, convictions, and ability to communicate authentically.

Questions for Reflection

Describe what "heal" means to you.

When were you last surprised, challenged, or touched? Explain.

How has becoming aware of your body's responses helped you address a pattern in yourself?

Explain the difference between joy and happiness as it applies to your life.

In what ways could you broaden or increase the love you express to others?

What action or activity could bring greater balance to your life?

Chapter 10

Touching the Essence of You

> "*Life shrinks or expands in proportion to one's courage.*"

— ANAIS NIN

Today, we are drowning in a lack of authenticity. We live in a world scarred with violence, political suppression, economic slavery, rampant narcissism, and human degradation, not to mention the threat of a nuclear war. Being shot is a possibility while shopping in a mall or relaxing in a theatre. The current global pandemic is a reality. We also experience constant noise, congestion, and traffic, the profound effect of which on our nervous system is often ignored or not even realized.

Who can we believe anymore? Our government representatives supposedly have an obligation to represent their constituents. However, they often get lost in political power struggles and appeasing the interests of big business. We find the FDA has approved drugs later shown to be dangerous, ones their manufacturers knew could be harmful. More and more TV shows reflect the upside of lying and manipulation. Advertisers will say almost anything to sell their products, whether it's true or not. In such circumstances, we naturally begin to question everything and everyone.

How many relationships have been built on false premises, where patterns of pleasing took precedence over the need for genuine connection? The desire to be loved became more important than respecting the true self's authenticity. The need to be needed prevented the real person from emerging. When did the fear of criticism, or even isolation, begin to keep people from expressing their truths? Social media "likes" and "shares" have become more important than genuine intimacy with the people we know. The overwhelming lack of authenticity I see everywhere in our world inspired me to write this book. For the sake of my own authenticity, I had to take action to create a clear, concise, and workable remedy for this lack in our humanity.

Imagine a world where authenticity drives our actions. A world where we could believe what we read, what people tell us, what we see on TV. We could watch the news, knowing reporters truly aimed to present all the facts without bias. Companies would strive to give the highest consideration to our environment and the general public, not just their investors and the bottom line. We could breathe fresh air and drink clean water. Our stress levels would go down drastically as the drive to push, hustle, and dominate would calm. Choices we make would be based on our heart's deepest desire, not the need to please others or simply survive.

I don't pretend that creating this world will be easy. To create it, we will need to change many things. And change can feel scary. It can stir up the fear of losing control, of losing safety, of losing what I have, or of not getting what I want. The brain is wired to relate to and recreate what it already knows. When things change, the first impulse is often to grip tight to all that is familiar. For some, change can be uncomfortable; for others, it is invigorating. Some souls are constantly seeking new revelations and answers to assist their growth on every level.

Change is happening constantly; it is the nature of life. Moving in sync with it is one of the greatest exercises of the human spirit. Delving deeply into our innermost thoughts and reflecting honestly on our actions can be an immense challenge, but it is one with a great reward. Are you willing to let your ideas of yourself change? Are you willing to give up what you have or who you are to become what you are not yet?

"Holding onto something that is good for you now may be the very reason why you don't have something better."

— C. JOY BELL

We are at a crisis point. All of humanity is staring at a moment when we must change. Our future depends on it. Fortunately, the path forward is simple, yet not always easy. Each of us, in each of our own personal lives, must commit to authenticity.

Authenticity is a collection of choices we must make every day. It's about the choice to show up and be real—the choice to be honest. The choice to let our true selves be seen. We can choose to surrender to our fears and continue on the road of familiar patterns, thereby obstructing our next step forward toward wholeness. Or we can refuse to accept the status quo we see around us and insist on celebrating and supporting a more authentic way of being.

"The key to changing the world, to changing your life, and to empowering those around you is authenticity."

— PANACHE DESAI

I love what author Barbara Brown Taylor has to say about life and change:

> I think we'd like life to be a train. You get on, pick your destination, and get off when you reach it. But life actually turns out to be a sailboat instead. Every day you have to see where the wind is and check the currents and see if there's anybody else on the boat with you who can help out. The currents change, and

so does the wind. It's not a train ride, in other words. It's not all about the destination, especially if the destination becomes an excuse for dismissing life now. That's a waste of a day, if not a life.

In other words, the work of authenticity never ends. Even when you have begun, you can find yourself falling back into old patterns and outmoded beliefs. As new ideas and experiences present themselves, authenticity calls for new responses. Making the commitment to change your core beliefs takes vigilance and commitment.

Why is authenticity important? What are the benefits? It seems like it takes a lot of work to accomplish being authentic while it also has the potential to be quite painful when identifying patterns, examining qualities, and figuring out what you truly believe. In addition to all of this, let's not forget the healing aspect.

The obvious reason to be authentic is to create a better world. As you look at the world today, you may feel discouraged. Our ravaged planet and harrowing lifestyle can feel overwhelming and impossible to change. However, doing nothing will leave us with only regret. One of the greatest benefits of taking action toward change is the opportunity to learn to know yourself, really know who you are as an individual. When you are comfortable in your own skin, and own it, you will begin to find value in your own individuality. Very few people really know themselves on a deep level.

Begin to nurture your own values and live your life accordingly. You will discover a greater sense of freedom in all your endeavors. The more powerfully you strive to live authentically, the greater the meaning and value of your life becomes. This end may sound rather self-centered and ego-driven; however, it is just the opposite. As you become aware of your patterns and live from the qualities rather than old patterns, a new sense of self will begin to emerge. This new self appreciates and values the person you have become.

The authentic goal is to live according to the guidance of your soul and spirit rather than ego. This results in being more open-hearted and patient. The freedom you will achieve opens up new horizons, new experiences, and new challenges. Courage replaces fear, and life becomes more meaningful at every turn. There is so much beauty when we are able to express the fullness of who we are. We are then able to attract so much joy and love into our lives and more fully enjoy others' authenticity.

As I observe our world and our culture, I think greater true authenticity would be such a fresh and uplifting change. We live in a world of many injustices: to humans, animals, and the planet. Will we have the courage to say "No" to the abusive, destructive behavior of others? "No" to pollution on the planet? And will we then say "Yes" to authentic, wholehearted living for the good of all? Will we be able to persist in the pursuit of telling the truth, even though we may experience rejection? The world and the very depths of our beings yearn for our genuine, authentic person to show up.

We want these "real" people to be our friends, our politicians, our doctors, and our teachers. This work is an investment of time, energy, and reflective thought. Not only as individuals do we need to stand up for our values and principles, but we need to encourage others to do the same. A world that supports the values of liberty, justice, and equality, where separateness is superseded by unity and competition is replaced by cooperation. This world will emerge when the entire collective practices authenticity.

"The future of humanity does not rest on one person, leader, or messiah with a greater consciousness to show us the way. Rather, it requires the evolution of a new collective consciousness, because it is through the acknowledgment and application of the interconnectedness of human consciousness that we can change the course of history."

— DR. JOE DISPENZA

I so encourage you to use this book as a guide on your journey to an authentic life. Answer the questions thoughtfully and honestly. You can return to the principles in this book over and over again to remind yourself how to expand into an even greater authentic life. Meditate to become in touch with your soul, the truest essence of you. Celebrate you!

What is the greatest gift you can give yourself and others?

"Every great dream begins with a dreamer. Always remember, you have within you the strength, the patience, and the passion to reach for the stars to change the world and yourself."

— HARRIET TUBMAN

MYSELF

I have to live with myself and so
I want to be fit for myself to know.
I want to be able as days go by,
Always to look myself straight in the eye;
I don't want to stand with the setting sun
And hate myself for the things I have done.

I don't want to keep on a closet shelf
A lot of secrets about myself
And fool myself as I come and go
Into thinking no one else will ever know
The kind of person I really am,
I don't want to dress up myself in sham.

I want to go out with my head erect
I want to deserve all men's respect;
But here in the struggle for fame and wealth
I want to be able to like myself.
I don't want to look at myself and know
I am bluster and bluff and empty show.

I never can hide myself from me;
I see what others may never see;
I know what others may never know,
I never can fool myself and so,
Whatever happens I want to be
Self-respecting and conscience free.

— Edgar A. Guest

A Final Note

"To become conscious and aware, we must become authentic. Authenticity is the highest form of being."

— TEAL SWAN

I wish to conclude this book with my truth. My *"True Self"* is the deepest part of my soul—the Divine spark within. This is the most pure, the most loving, and the kindest part of my being. It is perfection personified. It is the part of me from which miracles happen.

The work of the authentic self, as presented in this book, continues to be my path to access the essence of who I am, my *True Self, My God Self*. It is my fervent hope that this book will help you, the reader and architect of your life, find what is uniquely authentic to you. I desire that you come to know the joy and peace of living your most loving, true, and beautiful life. I believe we are each called to awaken this part of us and to live our lives as God intended at the time of our creation. Living a life of authentic expression, through all of its rich and various manifestations, is the way we are meant to navigate life's ups and downs and is possible for absolutely everyone.

I believe the investment of time required to consider, answer, and reflect on the questions posed in this book will bring you a life of incredible joy and freedom. I know, as you uncover your many gifts and talents, that you will love yourself more each day and that you will come to realize what a true gift you are to the world.

My best wishes in your pursuit of living your authenticity at your best!

Ann Allen

About the Author

Ann Allen is an author, therapist, keynote speaker, entrepreneur, and spiritual mentor. She received a Bachelor of Science from the University of Missouri in special education and taught orthopedically challenged children in a progressive educational system in Champaign, Illinois. This particular educational system caught her interest because the challenged students were integrated into the regular classroom as frequently as possible. She later received a master's degree from California State University with a major in biofeedback and wholistic health.

Ann has been in private practice for the past thirty-five years and has consulted many clients with regard to their health, stress management, and pain management. She utilizes biofeedback, reiki, Neuro-Link, and energy therapy to facilitate healing. For fifty years, she has sought the expansion of her own personal growth, studying with various deeply insightful spiritual teachers along the way.

After developing a successful workshop to help others obtain knowledge on the true meaning of authenticity and how to live authentically, she was guided to write this book.

Ann continues to honor and support the spiritual growth of her clients as she constantly seeks new templates of healing and spiritual expansion to examine. She passionately encourages the embodiment of each individual's unique and unlimited potential according to their unique Divine blueprint.

Ann lives in Littleton, Colorado.

About Ann Allen's Coaching

Ann Allen has been professionally engaged in assisting others to heal physically, emotionally, and spiritually for the past thirty-five years. Her joy effervesces when mentoring others in achieving their goals to experience life in a more healthy and joy-filled way. When working with her personally, you will receive the guidance and encouragement necessary to live authentically even in the most difficult circumstances.

Please contact Ann for a complimentary thirty-minute conversation to discuss how she might help you.

AnnAllenBook@gmail.com
720-593-9505
AuthenticityAtYourBest.com

Book Ann Allen to Speak at Your Next Event

Ann will inspire your audience to grasp the full value of living life authentically and expressing their true selves. You will learn what prevents living authentically as well as the qualities you must develop to achieve this goal. You will learn about the pitfalls that arise when life presents you with opportunities to express authentically and how to deal with them. Ann will encourage your audience to explore their dreams and passions to bring greater joy, freedom, and love into their lives.

Please contact Ann to discuss how she might help you.

AnnAllenBook@gmail.com